ACTIVITY & TEST PREP WORKBOOK

SIDE by SIDE

THIRD EDITION

BOOK 3

Steven J. Molinsky • Bill Bliss

with

Carolyn Graham

Contributing Authors

Dorothy Lynde • Elizabeth Handley

Illustrated by

Richard E. Hill

TO THE TEACHER

This enhanced edition of *Side by Side Activity Workbook 3* provides all-skills activities, lifeskills lessons, and achievement tests to reinforce, expand, and assess the learning objectives in the *Side by Side 3* and *Side by Side Plus 3* Student Books. It includes two audio CDs and an answer key, providing students with the resources they need to extend their language learning through self-study outside the classroom. The audio CDs contain all workbook listening activities and GrammarRaps that motivate learners and promote language mastery through entertaining practice with rhythm, stress, and intonation.

The achievement tests in the second section of the workbook (pages T1–T54) provide intensified coverage of lifeskill competencies, assess student progress, and prepare students for the types of standardized tests and performance assessments used by many instructional programs. The tests include: multiple-choice questions that assess vocabulary, grammar, reading, listening skills, lifeskill competencies, and basic literacy tasks (such as reading classified ads, signs, and everyday documents); writing assessments that can be evaluated using a standardized scoring rubric and collected in portfolios of students' work; and speaking performance assessments designed to stimulate face-to-face interactions between students, for evaluation by the teacher using a standardized scoring rubric, or for self-evaluation by students. Test pages are perforated so that completed tests can be handed in and can serve as a record of students' participation and progress in the instructional program.

Listening scripts and answer keys for the tests are provided in *Side by Side Plus* Teacher's Guide 3. Test preparation strategies, scoring rubrics, and resources for documenting students' progress are provided in *Side by Side Plus* Multilevel Activity & Achievement Test Book 3 and its accompanying CD-ROM.

Side by Side, 3rd edition
Activity & Test Prep Workbook 3

Copyright © 2009 by Prentice Hall Regents
Addison Wesley Longman, Inc.
A Pearson Education Company.
All rights reserved.
No part of this publication may be reproduced, stored in a
retrieval system, or transmitted in any form or by any
means, electronic, mechanical, photocopying, recording,
or otherwise, without the prior permission of the publisher.

Pearson Education, 10 Bank Street, White Plains, NY
10606
Editorial director: *Pam Fishman*
Vice president, director of design and production:
Rhea Banker
Director of electronic production:
Aliza Greenblatt
Production manager: *Ray Keating*
Director of manufacturing: *Patrice Fraccio*
Associate digital layout manager: *Paula Williams*

Associate art director: *Elizabeth Carlson*
Interior design: *Elizabeth Carlson, Wendy Wolf*
Cover design: *Elizabeth Carlson, Warren Fischbach*

The authors gratefully acknowledge the contribution
of Tina Carver in the development of the original
Side by Side program.

Printed in the United States of America
ISBN 978-0-13-040649-1; 0-13-040649-X

1 2 3 4 5 6 7 8 9 10 – CRK – 14 13 12 11 10 09

Contents

*Listening scripts and answer keys for the achievement tests are provided in *Side by Side Plus* Teacher's Guide 3.

what	bake	cook	move	sit
where	compose	go	read	watch

1. A. _____What's_____ Fran _____reading_____?

    B. _____She's reading_____ her e-mail.

2. A. _____Where's_____ Fred _go ing_?

    B. _He is going_ to the clinic.

3. A. _what's_ Nancy _doing_?

    B. _She is watching_ a game show.

4. A. _what are_ you _doing_?

    B. _I'm cooking_ dinner.

5. A. _where_ _what's are_ you and your wife _doing moving_?

    B. _we going_ to Miami.

6. A. _what's are_ your grandmother and grandfather _doing_?

    B. _Th are_ in the park.

7. A. _what's_ Victor _doing_?

    B. _He is compose_ a symphony.

8. A. _what are_ you _doing_?

    B. _I am baking_ an apple pie.

B ON THE PHONE

1. A. Hi. What ____are____ you doing?

   B. ____I'm watching____ a movie on TV.

   A. Oh. I don't want to disturb you. _____ Anna busy?

   B. Yes, _____. _____ a bath.

   A. I'll call back later.

2. A. Hi, Bill. _____ the children okay?

   B. Yes. _____ fine.

   A. What _____ doing?

   B. Vicky _____ her homework, and

      Timmy _____ baseball in the yard.

   A. How about you? _____ doing?

   B. _____ dinner for you and the kids.

   A. I'll be home soon.

3. A. Hello, Peter. This is Mr. Taylor. _____ your father
      at home?

   B. No, _____. _____ at the
      health club.

   A. Can I speak to your mother?

   B. I'm sorry. _____ busy right now. _____
      the washing machine. It's broken.

   A. Okay. I'll call back later.

4.
   A. Hello, _____. Can I speak to _____?

   B. I'm sorry. _____.

   A. Well, can I speak to _____?

   B. I'm afraid _____.

   A. Okay. I'll call back later.

1. *(clean)* I never _____clean_____ my apartment, but _____I'm cleaning_____ it today because __my grandmother is going to visit me (or) my boss is coming over for dinner__ .

2. *(iron)* Roger never _____ his shirts, but _____ them today because _____ .

3. *(argue)* We never _____ with our landlord, but _____ with him today because _____ .

4. *(worry)* I never _____ about anything, but _____ today because

   _____ .

5. *(watch)* Betty never _____ the news, but _____ it today because

   _____ .

6. *(write)* Uncle Phil never _____ to us, but _____ to us today because _____ .

7. *(take)* I never _____ the bus, but _____ it today because

   _____ .

8. *(comb)* My son never _____ his hair, but _____ it today because _____ .

9. *(get up)* My daughter never _____ early, but _____ early today because _____ .

10. *(smile)* Mr. Grimes never _____ , but _____ today because

    _____ .

11. *(bark)* Our dogs never _____ , but _____ today because _____ .

12. *(wear)* Alice never _____ perfume, but _____ it today because _____ .

1. I recommend the fish.   ___Do you recommend___ the chicken, too?

2. My husband bakes delicious cakes.   _____ he _____ pies, too?

3. My daughter gets up early.   _____ your son _____ early, too?

4. They always complain about the traffic.   _____ they _____ about the weather, too?

5. Maria speaks Italian and Spanish.   _____ she _____ French, too?

6. My grandson lives in Miami.   _____ your granddaughter _____ there, too?

7. I watch the news every morning.   _____ every evening, too?

8. My sister plays soccer.   _____ tennis, too?

9. Robert practices the trombone at night.   _____ during the day, too?

10. We plant vegetables every year.   _____ flowers, too?

11. Stanley always adds salt to the stew.   _____ pepper, too?

12. I always wear a jacket to work.   _____ a tie, too?

13. My cousin Sue rides a motorcycle.   _____ a bicycle, too?

14. My grandfather jogs every day.   _____ when it rains?

15. We need bread from the supermarket.   _____ milk, too?

16. Gregory always irons his shirts.   _____ his pants, too?

17. Our neighbors have three dogs.   _____ any cats?

Across

3. I like to cook. I'm an excellent _____.
4. I can type. I'm a very good _____.
5. Sally swims fast. She's a fast _____.
6. Jeff likes to play sports. He's a good
   _____.
7. My sons drive taxis. They're both taxi
   _____.

Down

1. You ski well. You're a very good _____.
2. We act in plays and movies. We're _____.
5. My children love to skate They're
   wonderful _____.

F **WHAT'S THE ANSWER?**

Circle the correct answer.

1. Does Hector like to play tennis?
   a. Yes, he likes.
   b. Yes, he does.
   c. Yes, he is.

2. Are you a graceful dancer?
   a. No, I don't.
   b. No, you aren't.
   c. No, I'm not.

3. Does your boss work hard?
   a. Yes, he is.
   b. Yes, he does.
   c. Yes, he works.

4. Is the food at this restaurant spicy?
   a. Yes, it isn't.
   b. Yes, it does.
   c. Yes, it is.

5. Are your children good athletes?
   a. Yes, I am.
   b. Yes, they are.
   c. Yes, they do.

6. Do you and your girlfriend like to cook?
   a. Yes, she does.
   b. Yes, they do.
   c. Yes, we do.

7. Am I a good teacher?
   a. Yes, you are.
   b. Yes, he is.
   c. Yes, you do.

8. Does your husband send e-mail messages to you?
   a. Yes, he is.
   b. Yes, he does.
   c. Yes, she does.

G WHAT ARE THEY SAYING?

1. A. I ____don't____ like to eat at Albert's house because he _____ cook very well.

   B. I know. Everybody says he _____ a very good _____.

2. A. I know you _____ like to drive with me because you think _____ a terrible driver.

   B. That's not true. I think you _____ very carefully!

3. A. _____ like to type?

   B. No, I _____. _____ not a very accurate typist.

   A. I disagree. _____ an accurate typist, but you _____ very slowly.

4. A. Oliver Jones is an excellent composer.

   B. I agree. He _____ beautifully. I think _____ very talented.

5. A. Irene _____ going swimming with us today because she _____ like to swim when it's cold.

   B. That's too bad. I really like to go swimming with her. She's a very good _____.

6. A. I'm jealous of my classmates. They speak English very well, and I _____.

   B. That's not true. Your classmates _____ English clearly, but you're a good

   English _____, too.

H LISTENING

Listen to each question and then complete the answer.

1. Yes, ____he does____.
2. No, ____she isn't____.
3. Yes, _____.
4. Yes, _____.
5. No, _____.
6. Yes, _____.
7. No, _____.
8. Yes, _____.
9. No, _____.
10. Yes, _____.
11. No, _____.
12. Yes, _____.
13. Yes, _____.
14. No, _____.
15. No, _____.

Listen. Then clap and practice.

A. Does he like   the movies?

B.   No,   he doesn't.   He likes   TV.

A. Does she like   the mountains?

B.   No,   she doesn't.   She likes   the sea.

A. Do you like to   hike?

B.   No,   I don't.   I like to   dive.

A. Do they like to   walk?

B.   No,   they don't.   They like to   drive.

A. Is he studying   music?

B.   No,   he isn't.   He's studying   math.

A. Is she taking   a shower?

B.   No,   she isn't.   She's taking   a bath.

A. Are they living   in Brooklyn?

B.   No,   they aren't. They're living   in Queens.

A. Are you washing   your shirt?

B.   No,   I'm not.   I'm washing   my jeans.

WHAT'S THE QUESTION?

1. We're waiting for <u>the bus</u>. _____ *What are you waiting for?* _____

2. He's thinking about <u>his girlfriend</u>. _____ *Who is he thinking about?* _____

3. They're ironing <u>their shirts</u>. _____

4. I'm calling <u>my landlord</u>. _____

5. She's dancing with <u>her father</u>. _____

6. He's watching <u>the news</u>. _____

7. They're complaining about <u>the rent</u>. _____

8. She's playing baseball with <u>her son</u>. _____

9. They're visiting <u>their cousins</u>. _____

10. We're looking at <u>the animals in the zoo</u>. _____

11. I'm writing about <u>my favorite movie</u>. _____

12. He's arguing with <u>his boss</u>. _____

13. She's knitting a sweater for <u>her daughter</u>. _____

14. We're making <u>pancakes</u>. _____

15. I'm sending an e-mail to <u>my uncle</u>. _____

16. They're worrying about <u>their examination</u>. _____

17. She's talking to <u>the soccer coach</u>. _____

18. He's skating with <u>his grandparents</u>. _____

1. A. Where are you and your husband taking _____your_____ children?

   B. _We're_ taking ___them___ to the zoo.

2. A. Why is Richard calling all _____ friends today?

   B. _____ wants to tell _____ about _____ new car.

3. A. What are your parents going to give you for your birthday?

   B. I'm not sure, but _____ might give _____ a puppy.

4. A. Why is Susie visiting _____ grandparents?

   B. _____ wants to show ___them___ her new bicycle.

5. A. Why are you wearing a safety helmet on _____your_____ head?

   B. ____I____ don't want to hurt _____my_____ head while I'm skateboarding.

6. A. Where are you taking _____ new girlfriend on Saturday night?

   B. ___I'm___ taking ___her___ to see the new science fiction movie downtown.

7. A. Why are those students complaining about their teacher?

   B. ___they___ think she gives ___them___ too much homework.

8. A. Can I tell you and Dad about the party now?

   B. No. We're sleeping now. You can tell ___us___ about ___it___ tomorrow morning.

9. A. Why is Mrs. Jenkins waiting for the plumber?

   B. The sink is leaking. Charlie, the plumber, says ___he___ can fix ___it___.

10. A. Timmy, why are you arguing with _____your_____ sister?

    B. ___She___ wants to play with _____my_____ new toys, but she can't. They're mine.

1. You should never argue
   at
   to
   (with)
   a police officer.

2. We're watching
   at
   to
   —
   a game show on TV.

3. You shouldn't shout
   (at)
   to
   —
   people.

4. Do you write
   at
   (to)
   from
   your keypals very often?

5. They always complain
   at
   —
   (about)
   the weather.

6. We visit
   at
   to
   —
   our sister's friends in Texas once a year.

7. I'm helping
   at
   to
   —
   my neighbors
   to
   (with)
   —
   their garden.

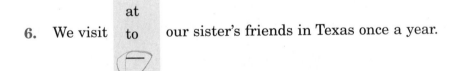

8. I'm always frustrated when I have to wait
   (for)
   —
   at
   the bus.

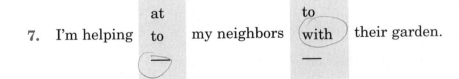

9. Call
   to
   —
   at
   the exterminator right away!

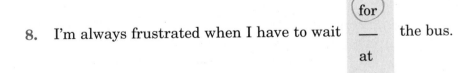

Herbert (have) ____had__¹ a very bad day yesterday. He usually gets up early, but yesterday

morning he (get up) _____² very late! He (eat) _____³ breakfast quickly,

(rush) _____⁴ out of the house, and (run) _____⁵ to the bus stop. Unfortunately, he

(miss) _____⁶ the bus. He (wait) _____⁷ for ten minutes, but there weren't

any more buses, so he (decide) _____⁸ to walk to his office. Herbert was upset. He

(arrive) _____⁹ at work two and a half hours late!

Herbert (sit) _____¹⁰ down at his desk and (begin) _____¹¹ his work. He

(call) _____¹² a few people on the telephone, and he (type) _____¹³ a few letters.

But he was in a hurry, and he (make) _____¹⁴ a lot of mistakes. He (fix) _____¹⁵

the mistakes, but when he (finish) _____¹⁶ the letters and (put) _____¹⁷ them on

his desk, he (spill) _____¹⁸ water all over them.

At noon, Herbert (go) _____¹⁹ to the company cafeteria and (order) _____²⁰ a

pizza for lunch. That was a big mistake. The pizza was very spicy, and Herbert (feel) _____²¹

sick for the rest of the day.

Herbert's afternoon was even worse than his morning. He (forget) _____²² about an

important meeting, his computer (crash) _____²³, he (fall) _____²⁴ asleep at his

desk, his chair (break) _____²⁵, and he (hurt) _____²⁶ his arm.

Herbert (leave) _____²⁷ the office at 5:00, (take) _____²⁸ the bus home, and

immediately (go) _____²⁹ to bed! What a terrible, terrible day!

B LISTENING

Listen and circle the correct answer.

1. yesterday **(every day)**	4. yesterday every day	7. yesterday every day	10. yesterday every day
2. **(yesterday)** every day	5. yesterday every day	8. yesterday every day	11. yesterday every day
3. yesterday every day	6. yesterday every day	9. yesterday every day	12. yesterday every day

C WHAT'S THE WORD?

Fill in the missing words. Then read the story aloud.

decide	lift	need	paint	plant	roller-blade	wait	want

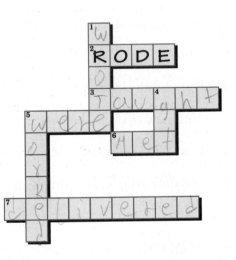

Last Saturday everyone __wanted__ [1] my help. In the morning, I
__lifted__ [2] heavy furniture for my wife, and I __painted__ [3] the
bathroom walls. Then I __roller-bladed__ [4] in the park with my son and
__planted__ [5] flowers with my daughter. In the afternoon, my brother
__needed__ [6] my help. I went to a store with him and __waited__ [7]
while he __decided__ [8] which suit to buy for his wedding.

D PUZZLE: *What Did They Do?*

Across
2. ride
3. teach
5. are
6. meet
7. deliver

Down
1. write
4. get
5. work

Activity Workbook   13

1. _____Did you buy_____ the green one?   No, I didn't. I bought the blue one.

2. _____ a plane?   No, they didn't. They took a boat.

3. _____ a movie?   No, she didn't. She saw a play.

4. _____ French?   No, he didn't. He spoke Arabic.

5. _____ your arm?   No, I didn't. I broke my leg.

6. _____ at seven?   No, it didn't. It began at eight.

7. _____ to Paris?   No, she didn't. She flew to Rome.

8. _____ the beef?   No, we didn't. We had the chicken.

9. _____ with you?   No, they didn't. They went alone.

10. _____ too softly?   No, you didn't. You sang too loudly.

11. _____ your mother?   No, he didn't. He met my father.

12. _____ your keys?   No, I didn't. I lost my ring.

F WHAT'S THE ANSWER?

was	were		angry	hungry	prepared	scared	tired
wasn't	weren't		bored	on time	sad	thirsty	

1. The students fell asleep in Professor Winter's class because _____they were bored_____.

2. I didn't finish my sandwich today because _____I wasn't hungry_____.

3. They went to bed early last night because _____they were tired_____.

4. She didn't do well on the test because _____she wasn't prepared_____.

5. He shouted at them because _____he was angry_____.

6. I missed the train this morning because _____I wasn't on time_____.

7. My daughter didn't finish all her milk because _____she wasn't thirsty_____.

8. I covered my eyes during the movie because _____I was scared_____.

9. They cried when they said good-bye at the airport because _____they were sad_____.

G SOMETHING DIFFERENT

1. Albert usually drives very carefully.

   He ___didn't drive___ carefully yesterday afternoon.

   He ___drove___ much too fast.

2. Alice usually comes home from work early.

   She ___didn't come___ home early last night.

   She ___came___ home late.

3. I usually take the bus to work.

   I ___didn't take___ the bus this morning.

   I ___took___ the train.

4. We usually go to the movies on Saturday.

   We _____ to the movies last Saturday.

   We _____ to a concert.

5. Carl and Tom usually forget their homework.

   They _____ their homework yesterday.

   They _____ their lunch.

6. Mr. Tyler usually wears a suit to the office.

   He _____ a suit today.

   He _____ jeans.

7. Professor Hall usually teaches biology.

   She _____ biology last semester.

   She _____ astronomy.

8. Mr. and Mrs. Miller usually eat dinner at 7:00.

   They _____ dinner at 7:00 last night.

   They _____ at 9:00.

9. My grandmother usually gives me a tie for my birthday.

   She _____ me a tie this year.

   She _____ me a watch.

10. Alan usually sits by himself in English class.

    He _____ by himself today.

    He _____ with all his friends.

11. I usually have cereal for breakfast.

    I _____ cereal this morning.

    I _____ eggs.

12. Amanda usually sings very beautifully.

    She _____ beautifully last night.

    She _____ very badly.

1. A. _____Did you_____ clean your apartment this week?

   B. No, I ___didn't___. I ___was___ too lazy.

2. A. _____ meet the company president at the office party?

   B. No, we _____. But we _____ his wife.

3. A. _____ Richard fall?

   B. Yes, he _____. He skated very quickly, and he _____ very careful.

4. A. _____ Rita deliver all the pizzas today?

   B. No, _____. The people at 10 Main Street _____ home.

5. A. _____ Roger _____ asleep at the meeting this morning?

   B. No, _____. But he ___fell___ asleep later in his office. He ___was___ very tired.

6. A. ___did___ you ride your motorcycle to work today?

   B. No, _____. I ___rode___ my bicycle, and I ___was___ late. My supervisor ___was___ upset.

7. A. ___Did___ like the movie?

    B. Yes, I ___did___. It ___was___ great! How about you? Did you like it?

    A. No, I ___didn't___. I thought it ___was___ boring.

8. A. ___Was___ Mrs. Sanchez your Spanish teacher last semester?

    B. Yes, she _____. ___Were___ you in her class?

    A. No, ___wasn't___. I ___didn't___ take Spanish. I took French.

9. A. ___did___ you complain to your landlord about the problems in your apartment?

    B. Yes, we ___did___. He listened to us, but he ___didn't___ fix anything. We _____ very angry.

10. A. ___did___ the students dance gracefully in the school play?

    B. No, ___they didn't___. They ___danced___ very awkwardly. They ___were___ very nervous.

11. A. Dad, ___Did___ you buy anything at the supermarket?

    B. Yes, ___I did___. I ___bought___ some food for dinner.

    A. ___Did you___ buy any ice cream?

    B. Sorry. I ___didn't___. There ___weren't___ any.

12. A. Grandpa, ___were___ you a good soccer player when you ___were___ young?

    B. Yes, ___I was___. I ___was___ a very good player. I ___was___ fast, and I ___wasn't___ clumsy.

1. How did Steven sprain his ankle? *(play tennis)*

   _____ He sprained his ankle while he was playing tennis. _____

2. How did your sister rip her pants? *(exercise)*

   _____

3. How did you break your arm? *(play volleyball)*

   _____

4. How did James poke himself in the eye? *(fix his sink)*

   _____

5. How did you and your brother hurt yourselves? *(skateboard)*

   _____

6. How did Mr. and Mrs. Davis trip and fall? *(dance)*

   _____

7. How did your father burn himself? *(cook french fries)*

   _____

8. How did your daughter get a black eye? *(fight with the kid across the street)*

   _____

9. How did you cut yourself? *(chop carrots)*

   _____

10. How did Robert lose his cell phone? *(jog in the park)*

    _____

11. How did you _____?

    _____

J GRAMMARRAP: *What Did He Do?*

Listen. Then clap and practice.

A.   What did he   do?

B.   He did   his homework.

A.   What did she   sing?

B.   She sang   a song.

A.   What did they   hide?

B.   They hid   their money.

A.   Where did you   go?

B.   I went to   Hong Kong.

A.   What did he   lose?

B.   He lost his   watch.

A.   What did he   study?

B.   He studied   French.

A.   What did it   cost?

B.   It cost   a lot.

A.   What did they   buy?

B.   They bought   a wrench.

K GRAMMARRAP: *I Was Talking to Bob When I Ran Into Sue*

Listen. Then clap and practice.

I was talking to   Bob when   I ran into   Sue.

I was waiting for   Jack when   I saw   Mary Lou.

They were cleaning   the house when   I knocked on the door.

He was dusting   a lamp when   it fell   on the floor.

She was learning to   drive when   I met her   last May.

She was buying   a car when   I saw her   today.

How	What	Where
How long	What kind of	Who
How many	When	Why

1. _____Who did you meet?_____   I met the president.

2. ___what did she lose___   She lost her purse.

3. ___where did you do your exercises___ We did our exercises at the beach.

4. ___when did they leave___   They left at 9:15.

5. ___How did she get there___   She got here by plane.

6. ___Where did he sing?___   He sang in a concert hall.

7. ___How long did they stay?___   They stayed for a week.

8. ___what did you see?___   I saw a science fiction movie.

9. ___why did they cry?___   He cried because the movie was sad.

10. ___Who did she write a letter to?___ She wrote a letter to her brother.

11. ___what did they complain about?___ They complained about the telephone bill.

12. ___How many grapes did you eat?___ We ate a lot of grapes.

13. ___where did she speak?___   He spoke at the meeting.

14. ___How long did they lift weights?___ They lifted weights all morning.

15. ___who did she give a present to?___ She gave a present to her cousin.

16. ___what kind of pie did you order?___ I ordered apple pie.

17. ___How many videos did you rent?___ We rented seven videos.

18. ___who did they send an e-mail to?___ They sent an e-mail to their teacher.

19. ___when did he fall asleep?___   He fell asleep during the lecture.

20. ___when did you lose your hat___ I lost my hat while I was skiing.

1. A. Did you go to Hong Kong?

   B. No, ____we didn't____ .

   A. Where ____did you go____ ?

   B. ____We went____ to Tokyo.

2. A. Did you get there by boat?

   B. No, _____ .

   A. How _____ ?

   B. _____ .

3. A. Did your flight to Japan leave on time?

   B. No, ____it didn't____ .

   A. How late ____did it leave____ _____ ?

   B. ____it left____ two hours late.

4. A. Did you have good weather during the flight?

   B. No, _____ .

   A. What kind of _____ _____ ?

   B. _____ terrible weather.

5. A. Did you stay in a big hotel?

   B. No, _____ .

   A. What kind of _____ _____ ?

   B. _____ .

6. A. Did you eat American food?

   B. No, _____ .

   A. What kind of _____ _____ ?

   B. _____ .

(continued)

7. A. Did you take your camera with you?

    B. No, _____ .

    A. What _____

    _____ _____ ?

    B. _____ our camcorder.

8. A. Did you get around the city by train?

    B. No, _____ .

    A. How _____

    _____ ?

    B. _____ .

9. A. Did you meet many Japanese?

    B. No, _____ .

    A. Who _____ ?

    B. _____ other tourists.

10. A. Did you buy any clothing?

    B. No, _____ .

    A. What _____ ?

    B. _____ souvenirs.

Where's the train station?

11. A. Did you speak Japanese?

    B. No, _____ .

    A. What language _____

    _____ ?

    B. _____ .

12. A. Did you spend a lot of money?

    B. Yes, _____ .

    A. How much _____

    _____ ?

    B. ....

N SOUND IT OUT!

Listen to each word and then say it.

this				these		
1. chicken	3. river	5. busy		1. cheese	3. asleep	5. Steve
2. middle	4. kid	6. didn't		2. meat	4. receive	6. repeat

Listen and put a circle around the word that has the same sound.

1. clean:	fine	middle	(these)
2. mix:	ski	did	need
3. easy:	Rita	break	eyes
4. video:	machine	big	keep
5. east:	build	little	green
6. symphony:	mittens	life	retire
7. rip:	knee	maybe	knit

Now make a sentence using all the words you circled, and read the sentence aloud.

8. _____ _____ _____ _____ _____

_____ _____

9. meat:	Greek	Internet	eight
10. spill:	healthy	his	rainy
11. promise:	child	key	Richard
12. tea:	every	men	into
13. cookie:	with	speaks	bricks
14. milk:	mine	advice	with
15. team:	is	week	attractive
16. typical:	sister	lazy	rebuild

Now make a sentence using all the words you circled, and read the sentence aloud.

17. _____ _____ _____ _____ _____

_____ _____

A WHAT ARE THEY SAYING?

1. A. Did you ride your bicycle to work this morning?

   B. ___No, I didn't___ . I ___rode___ my

   motorcycle. ___I'm going to ride___ my bicycle to work tomorrow morning.

2. A. Did Tommy wear his new shoes to school today?

   B. _____. He _____

   his old shoes. _____
   his new shoes tomorrow.

3. A. Did Sally give her husband a sweater for his birthday this year?

   B. _____. She _____

   him a tie. _____
   him a sweater next year.

4. A. Did your parents drive to the mountains last weekend?

   B. _____. They _____ to

   the beach. _____
   to the mountains next weekend.

5. A. Did you and your family have eggs for breakfast this morning?

   B. _____. We _____

   pancakes. _____
   eggs tomorrow morning.

6. A. Did you go out with Mandy last Saturday night?

   B. _____. I _____

   out with Sandy. _____
   out with Mandy next Saturday night.

7. A. Did Howard write an interesting story for homework today?

   B. _____. He _____ a

   boring one. _____
   a more interesting story next time.

8. A. Did Shirley leave the office early this afternoon?

   B. _____. She _____

   very late. _____
   early tomorrow afternoon.

A 24   Activity Workbook

1. I'm really scared. Tomorrow my dentist is going to ##########.

I'm sorry. I can't hear you. I think we have a bad connection. What's _your dentist going to do_ ?

2. We're very excited about our trip. We're going to go to ##########.

What did you say? I can't hear you. Where _____ _____?

3. My son is very sad. His girlfriend is going to move to Alaska because ############.

I'm sorry. We have a bad connection. Why _____ _____?

4. My parents are going to give me a ########## for my sixteenth birthday.

Excuse me. I can't hear you. _____ _____?

5. I'm really nervous. I'm going to ########## for the first time tomorrow.

We have a bad connection. _____ _____?

6. Please come to our wedding. We're going to get married next ##########.

I'm sorry. I can't hear you. _____ _____?

7. I won't be home after school today. I'm going to meet ##########.

This is a terrible connection! _____ _____?

(continued)

Listen and choose the time of the action.

1. a. last night
   b. tomorrow night

2. a. yesterday afternoon
   b. tomorrow afternoon

3. a. this weekend
   b. last weekend

4. a. this Saturday
   b. last Saturday

5. a. last week
   b. next week

6. a. yesterday evening
   b. this evening

7. a. tomorrow night
   b. last night

8. a. this weekend
   b. last weekend

9. a. this evening
   b. yesterday evening

10. a. last winter
    b. this winter

11. a. tomorrow morning
    b. yesterday morning

12. a. next semester
    b. last semester

D THE PESSIMIST AND THE OPTIMISTS

James is a pessimist. He always thinks the worst will happen.

All his friends are optimists. They always tell James he shouldn't worry.

1. I'm afraid I ____won't have____ a good time at the office party tomorrow.

   Yes, ____you will____. ____You'll____ have a wonderful time.

2. I'm sure my son ____will hurt____ himself in his soccer match today.

   No, ____he won't____. ____He won't____ hurt himself. He's always very careful.

3. I'm afraid my grandmother ____won't____ get out of the hospital soon.

   Yes, ____she will____. ____she will____ get out of the hospital in a few days.

4. I'm afraid my wife _____ upset if I get a very short haircut.

   No, _____. _____ be upset.

5. I'm positive I ____won't lose____ weight on my new diet.

   Yes, ____you will____. ____you will____ lose a lot of weight.

6. I'm afraid my children _____ my birthday this year.

   No, _____. _____ forget your birthday. They never forget it.

7. I'm afraid my landlord _____ our broken doorbell.

   Yes, _____. _____ fix it as soon as he can.

8. I'm afraid my new neighbors _____ like me.

   Of course _____. _____ you a lot. Everybody likes you.

9. I'm sure _____ catch a cold when we go camping this weekend.

   No, _____. _____ catch a cold, James. You worry too much!

E WHAT WILL BE HAPPENING?

attend	browse	clean	do	fill out	rain	watch	work out

1. A. Will Amanda be busy this afternoon?

   B. Yes, ____she will____ .

   ____She'll be doing____ research at the library.

2. A. Will you be busy this evening?

   B. Yes, _____ . _____

   _____ my income tax form.

3. A. Will Donald be home this afternoon?

   B. No, _____ . _____

   _____ at his health club.

4. A. Will Mr. and Mrs. Lee be busy tonight?

   B. Yes, _____ . _____

   _____ their apartment.

5. A. Will Grandpa be busy tonight?

   B. Yes, _____ . _____

   _____ the web until after midnight.

6. A. Will you and your wife be home today?

   B. Yes, _____ . _____

   _____ our favorite game show on TV.

7. A. Will Mom be home early tonight?

   B. No, _____ . _____

   _____ a meeting.

8. A. Will the weather be nice this weekend?

   B. No, _____ . _____

   _____ cats and dogs!

28 Activity Workbook

F A TOUR OF MY CITY

Pretend you're taking people on a tour of your city or town. Fill in the blanks with real places you know.

Good morning, everybody. This is _____ speaking. I'm

so glad you'll be coming with me today on a tour of _____.

We'll be leaving in just a few minutes.

First, I'll be taking you to see my favorite places in the city: _____,

_____, and _____.

Then we'll be going to _____ for lunch. In my opinion, this is

the best restaurant in town. After that, I'll be taking you to see the other interesting

tourist sights: _____, _____,

and _____. This evening we'll be going to _____

_____. I'm sure you'll have a wonderful time.

G WHAT ARE THEY SAYING?

1. A. I'm sorry. I can't talk right now. I'm

   _____giving_____ the kids a bath.

   B. How much longer _will you be giving_
      them a bath?

2. A. How much longer _____

      _____ your homework?

   B. I'll probably _____
      my homework for another half hour.

   A. Okay. I'll call you then.

3. A. Hi, Carol. This is Bob. Can you

      _____ for a minute?

   B. Sorry. I can't _____ right now.

      I'm _____ for a big test.

4. A. Sorry, Alan. I can't talk now. I'm

      _____ dinner with my family.

   B. How much longer _____

      _____ dinner?

H GRAMMARRAP: *Will They Be Home?*

Listen. Then clap and practice.

A.   Will you   be home   at a quarter   to three?

B.   Yes,   I will.   I'll be watching   TV.

A.   Will John   be home   at half   past two?

B.   Yes,   he will.   He'll be cooking   some stew.

A. Will your parents   be home   today   at four?

B.   Yes,   they will.   They'll be washing   the floor.

A.   Will Jane   be home   if I call   at one?

B.   Yes,   she will.   She'll be feeding   her son.

A.   Will you   be home   at half   past eight?

B.   No,   I won't.   I'll be working   late.

A.   Will John   be home   at a quarter   to ten?

B.   No,   he won't.   He'll be visiting   a friend.

A. Will your parents   be home   tonight   at nine?

B.   No,   they won't.   They'll be standing   in line.

A.   Will Jane   be home   if I call her   at seven?

B.   No,   she won't.   She'll be dancing   with Kevin.

30   Activity Workbook

I WHOSE IS IT?

mine	his	hers	ours	yours	theirs

A. Hi, Robert. I found this wallet in my office today. Is it _____yours_____[1]?

B. No, it isn't _____[2], but it might be Tom's.

A. Maybe, but Tom hardly ever visits my office. It probably isn't _____[3].

B. It's small and blue. Maybe it's Martha's.

A. I asked her this morning. She says it isn't _____[4].

B. Is there anything inside the wallet?

A. There isn't any money, but there's a picture of three children.

B. It might belong to Mr. Hill. He and his wife have three children.

Maybe the children are _____[5].

A. I showed the picture to Mr. and Mrs. Hill. They said, "These

children aren't _____[6]. Our children are older."

B. Maybe you should give the wallet to our supervisor.

A. You know, it might be _____[7]. She has three children!

B. You're right. I'm positive it's _____[8]. I saw her children in her office last week.

J GRAMMARRAP: *Where's My Coat?*

Listen. Then clap and practice.

A. Where's my coat? I can't find mine.

Is this one mine or yours?

B. That one is mine. It isn't yours.

Yours is next to those doors.

A. Where's our umbrella? We can't find ours.

Is this one ours or theirs?

B. That one is theirs. It isn't yours.

Yours is under those chairs.

Circle the correct answer.

1. Jim is wearing a tuxedo today.
   a. He's going to visit his grandmother.
   b. He's going to a wedding.
   c. He's going to work in a factory.

2. My brother has a black eye.
   a. He painted his eye.
   b. He's wearing dark glasses.
   c. He hurt his eye.

3. The teacher wasn't on time.
   a. She was early.
   b. She was late.
   c. She didn't have a good time.

4. They chatted online yesterday.
   a. They used a cell phone.
   b. They used a computer.
   c. They used a fax machine.

5. Everyone in my family is going to relax this weekend.
   a. We're going to rest this weekend.
   b. We're going to retire this weekend.
   c. We're going to return this weekend.

6. He wasn't prepared for his exam.
   a. He didn't study for the exam.
   b. He didn't take the exam.
   c. He was ready for the exam.

7. Could I ask you a favor?
   a. I want to help you.
   b. I want to give you something.
   c. I need your help.

8. It's a very emotional day for Janet.
   a. She's going to work.
   b. She's getting married.
   c. She's studying.

9. He's composing a symphony.
   a. He's writing a symphony.
   b. He's listening to a symphony.
   c. He's going to a concert.

10. George ripped his shirt.
    a. He has to wash his shirt.
    b. He has to iron his shirt.
    c. He has to sew his shirt.

11. Can I borrow your bicycle?
    a. I need your bicycle for a little while.
    b. I want to give you my bicycle.
    c. I want to buy your bicycle.

12. Every day I practice ballet.
    a. I sing every day.
    b. I play violin every day.
    c. I dance every day.

13. I'm going to lend my car to Bob today.
    a. Bob is going to drive my car.
    b. I'm going to drive Bob's car.
    c. Bob is going to give me his car.

14. Mr. and Mrs. Hansen love to talk about their grandchildren.
    a. They listen to them.
    b. They're very proud of them.
    c. They argue with them.

15. Rita did very well on her exam.
    a. She's happy.
    b. She's anxious.
    c. She's sad.

16. I'm going to repair my washing machine.
    a. I'm going to paint it.
    b. I'm going to fix it.
    c. I'm going to do laundry.

17. I need to assemble my new VCR.
    a. Can I borrow your screwdriver?
    b. Can I borrow your ladder?
    c. Can I borrow your TV?

18. I sprained my ankle.
    a. I broke my ankle.
    b. I hurt my ankle.
    c. I poked my ankle.

19. I'm going to fill out my income tax form.
   a. I'm going to return it.
   b. I'm going to read it.
   c. I'm going to answer the questions on the form.

20. They're playing Scrabble.
   a. They're playing a game.
   b. They're playing a sport.
   c. They're playing an instrument.

21. Mr. Smith is complaining to his boss.
   a. He's talking about his boss, and he's upset.
   b. He's talking to his boss, and he's happy.
   c. He's talking to his boss, and he's upset.

22. I'm going to call my wife right away.
   a. I'm going to call her immediately.
   b. I'm going to call her in a few hours.
   c. I'm going to call her when I have time.

23. My sister is an excellent athlete.
   a. She's an active person.
   b. She plays sports very well.
   c. She likes to watch sports.

24. My mother is looking forward to her retirement.
   a. She's happy about her new job.
   b. She wants to buy new tires for her car.
   c. Soon she won't have to go to work every day.

LISTENING: *Looking Forward*

Listen to each story. Then answer the questions.

What Are Mr. and Mrs. Miller Looking Forward to?

1. Mr. and Mrs. Miller _____ last week.
   a. moved
   b. relaxed
   c. flew to Los Angeles

2. Mr. and Mrs. Miller aren't going to _____ this weekend.
   a. repaint their living room
   b. assemble their VCR
   c. relax in their yard

3. They're going to _____ next weekend.
   a. assemble their computer
   b. relax
   c. paint flowers

What's Jonathan Looking Forward to?

4. Jonathan isn't _____ today.
   a. sitting in his office
   b. thinking about his work
   c. thinking about next weekend

5. Next weekend he'll be _____.
   a. working
   b. cooking and cleaning
   c. getting married

6. On their trip to Hawaii, Jonathan and his wife won't be _____.
   a. swimming in the ocean
   b. paying bills
   c. eating in restaurants

What's Mrs. Grant Looking Forward to?

7. When she retires, Mrs. Grant will be _____.
   a. getting up early
   b. getting up late
   c. taking the bus to work

8. Mrs. Grant will _____ with her friends.
   a. go to museums
   b. work in her garden
   c. read books

9. She'll take her grandchildren to _____.
   a. the park and the beach
   b. the zoo and the beach
   c. the park and the zoo

✓ CHECK-UP TEST: Chapters 1–3

A. Fill in the blanks.

Ex. Ann ___is___ a good skater, and

her children __skate__ well, too.

1. A. Mr. and Mrs. Lee _____
   wonderful dancers.

   B. I agree with you. They

   _____ very well.

2. A. Roger _____ very
   carelessly.

   B. I know. He's a terrible driver.

3. A. We don't swim very well.

   B. I disagree. I think _____

   excellent _____.

4. A. I type very well. I think _____

   a very good _____.

5. A. We _____ good _____,
   but we like to ski anyway.

B. Fill in the blanks.

1. A. Did you speak to Mrs. Baxter
   yesterday?

   B. No, I _____. I _____

   too busy. But I _____ to Mrs.
   Parker.

2. A. Did you buy juice when you were at
   the store?

   B. No, I _____. I forgot. But

   I _____ milk.

3. A. _____ they get up early this
   morning?

   B. No, they _____. They _____
   up very late.

4. A. Did Mr. Wong teach biology last
   semester?

   B. No, he _____. He _____
   astronomy because the astronomy

   teacher _____ sick all semester.

5. A. _____ you talk to Tom last night?

   B. No, I _____. I _____ to
   his wife. Tom _____ there when
   I called.

C. Write the questions.

Ex. We're arguing with <u>our landlord</u>.

_____ *Who are you arguing with?* _____

1. I'm writing about <u>my favorite movie</u>.

   _____

2. They're going to fix <u>their bookcase</u>.

   _____

3. He hiked <u>in the mountains</u>.

   _____

4. She'll be ready <u>in a few minutes</u>.

   _____

5. They arrived <u>by plane</u>.

   _____

6. We'll be staying until <u>Monday</u>.

   _____

7. She's going to hire <u>five</u> people.

   _____

D. Answer the questions.

Ex. What did your daughter do yesterday morning?

(do her homework) _____ She did her homework. _____

1. What's your sister doing today?

   (adjust her satellite dish) _____

2. What does your brother do every evening?

   (chat online) _____

3. What are you going to do next weekend?

   (visit my mother-in-law) _____

4. What did Jack and Rick do yesterday afternoon?

   (deliver groceries) _____

5. What was David doing when his children came home from school?

   (bake a cake) _____

6. How will you get to work tomorrow?

   (take the bus) _____

7. What will you and your husband be doing this evening?

   (watch TV) _____

8. How did you cut your hand?

   (chop carrots) _____

E. Listen to each question and then complete the answer.

Ex. Yes, _____ he does _____.

1. Yes, _____.   5. No, _____.

2. No, _____.   6. Yes, _____.

3. Yes, _____.   7. No, _____.

4. Yes, _____.   8. Yes, _____.

A FOR MANY YEARS

1. I ride horses.

   ___I've ridden___ horses
   for many years.

2. I fly airplanes.

   _____ airplanes
   for several years.

3. I give injections at the hospital.

   _____ injections
   for many years.

4. I speak Italian.

   _____ it
   all my life.

5. I take photographs.

   _____ them
   for many years.

6. I do exercises every day.

   _____ them
   every day for many years.

7. I draw cartoons.

   _____ cartoons
   for several years.

8. I write for a newspaper.

   _____ for a
   newspaper for many years.

9. I drive carefully.

   _____ carefully
   all my life.

B LISTENING

Listen and choose the word you hear.

1. a. ridden
   b. written

2. a. taking
   b. taken

3. a. giving
   b. given

4. a. written
   b. driven

5. a. writing
   b. written

6. a. drawing
   b. doing

7. a. spoken
   b. speaking

8. a. done
   b. drawn

be	fly	give	ride	sing	take
draw	get	go	see	swim	write

1. _____I've never flown_____
in a helicopter.

2. _____
a raise.

3. _____
in a limousine.

4. _____
a cartoon.

5. _____
a book.

6. _____
a trip to Hawaii.

7. _____
in a choir.

8. _____
in the Mediterranean.

9. _____
on television.

10. _____
on a cruise.

11. _____
a present to my teacher.

12. _____
a Broadway show.

D LISTENING

Is Speaker B answering *Yes* or *No*? Listen to each conversation and circle the correct answer.

1. (Yes)   No   3. Yes   (No)   5. Yes   (No)   7. Yes   (No)

2. Yes   (No)   4. (Yes)   No   6. (Yes)   No   8. Yes   (No)

WHAT ARE THEY SAYING?

fall	get	give	go	ride	wear

1. A. _____Have you ever gotten_____ stuck in bad traffic?

   B. Yes. As a matter of fact, _____I got_____ stuck in very bad traffic this morning.

2. A. _____ on a Ferris wheel?

   B. Yes, I have. _____ on a Ferris wheel last weekend.

3. A. _____ a tuxedo?

   B. Yes, I have. _____ a tuxedo to my sister's wedding.

4. A. _____ scuba diving?

   B. Yes, I have. _____ scuba diving last summer.

5. A. _____ blood?

   B. Yes, I have. _____ blood a few months ago.

6. A. _____ on the sidewalk?

   B. Yes. In fact, _____ on the sidewalk a few days ago.

F **GRAMMARRAP:** *Have You Ever?*

Listen. Then clap and practice.

A. Have you ever   seen   a rainbow?

Have you ever   learned   to dance?

Have you ever   flown   an airplane?

Have you ever   gone   to France?

B. No, I've never   seen   a rainbow.

I've never   learned   to dance.

I've never   flown   an airplane.

But I've often   gone   to France.

WHAT ARE THEY SAYING?

drive	eat	go	meet	see	speak	take	write

1. A. __Have__ your children __eaten__ breakfast yet?

   B. Yes, __they have__ . __They ate__ breakfast a little while ago.

2. A. _____ George _____ his new car yet?

   B. Yes, _____ . _____ it for the first time this morning.

3. A. _____ Gloria _____ to the post office yet?

   B. Yes, _____ . _____ to the post office a little while ago.

4. A. _____ you and Jane _____ the new movie at the Westville Mall?

   B. Yes, _____ . _____ it last Saturday night.

5. A. _____ the employees _____ inventory yet?

   B. Yes, _____ . _____ inventory last weekend.

6. A. _____ you _____ to the landlord yet?

   B. Yes, _____ . _____ to him this morning.

7. A. _____ I _____ a letter to the Carter Company yet?

   B. Yes, _____ . _____ them a letter last week.

8. A. _____ you and your wife _____ your daughter's new boyfriend yet?

   B. Yes, _____ . _____ him last Friday night.

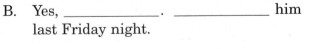

1. Kenji and his girlfriend aren't going to eat at Burger Town today. ___They've___ already ___eaten___ at Burger Town this week. ___They ate___ there on Monday.

2. My sister isn't going dancing tonight. ___she's___ already ___gone___ dancing this week. ___went___ dancing last night.

3. Timothy isn't going to wear his new jacket to work today. ___He's___ already ___worn___ it to work this week. ___He wore___ it yesterday.

4. My husband and I aren't going to do our laundry today. ___we're___ already ___done___ our laundry this week. ___we did___ it on Saturday.

5. Roger isn't going to give his girlfriend candy today. ___he's___ already ___given___ her candy this week. ___he gave___ her candy yesterday morning.

6. I'm not going to see a movie today. ___I've___ already ___seen___ a movie this week. ___Saw___ a movie on Wednesday.

7. We aren't going to buy fruit at the supermarket today. ___we've___ already ___bought___ fruit at the supermarket this week. ___we bought___ some fruit two days ago.

8. Susie isn't going to visit her grandparents today. ___She's___ already ___visited___ them this week. ___visited___ them yesterday.

9. David isn't going to take his children to the circus today. ___he's___ already ___taken___ them to the circus this week. ___he took___ them to the circus a few days ago.

❶ WHAT'S THE WORD?

go
went
gone

1. We should ____go____ now.

2. They ___went___ home early today.

3. She's already ___gone___ home.

see
saw
seen

4. I've never _____ him.

5. I _____ her yesterday.

6. Do you _____ them often?

eat
ate
eaten

7. I _____ there this morning.

8. Has he ever _____ there?

9. Do you _____ there every day?

write
wrote
written

10. How often do you _____ to them?

11. She's already _____ her report.

12. He _____ her a very long letter.

wear
wore
worn

13. When will you ___wear___ it?

14. He's never _____ it.

15. She _____ it today.

speak
spoke
spoken

16. Who _____ to you about it?

17. She can't _____ Chinese.

18. Have they _____ to you?

drive
drove
driven

19. They've never _____ there.

20. We never like to _____ there.

21. She _____ there today.

do
did
done

22. Did you ___do___ your homework?

23. We ___did___ that yesterday.

24. Have you ever ___done___ that?

1. A. Janet, you've got to do your homework.

   B. But, Mother, __I've__ already __done__ my homework today.

   A. Really? When?

   B. Don't you remember? __I did__ my homework this afternoon.

   A. Oh, that's right. Also, __have__ you __written__ a letter to Grandma yet?

   B. Yes, __have__. I wrote to her yesterday.

2. A. Would you like to swim at the health club tonight?

   B. I don't think so. _____ already _____ at the health club today.

   A. Really? When?

   B. __Swam__ there this morning.

3. A. Are you going to take your vitamins?

   B. _____ already _____ them.

   A. Really? When?

   B. __I took__ them before breakfast.
      How about you? __have__ you __taken__ yours?

   A. Yes, __I have__. I __took__ mine when I got up.

4. A. I hope Jimmy gets a haircut soon.

   B. Don't worry, Mother. __he's__ already __gotten__ one.

   A. I'm glad to hear that. When?

   B. __he got__ a haircut yesterday.

   A. That's wonderful!

5. A. When are you and Fred going to eat at the new restaurant downtown?

B. _____ we've _____ already _____ eaten _____ there.

A. Really? When?

B. _____ We ate _____ there last weekend.

A. How was the food?

B. It was terrible. It was the worst food we've ever _____ eaten _____!

6. A. When are you going to speak to the boss about a raise?

B. _____ I've _____ already _____ spoken _____ to her.

A. Really? When?

B. _____ I spoke _____ to her this morning.

A. What did she say?

B. She said, "_____."

K GRAMMARRAP: *Have You Gone to the Bank?*

Listen. Then clap and practice.

A. Have you gone to the   bank?

B.   Yes,   I have.
     I went to the   bank   at noon.

A. Have they taken   a vacation?

B.   Yes,   they have.
     They took   a vacation   in June.

A. Has he written   the letters?

B.   Yes,   he has.
     He wrote   the letters   today.

A. Has she gotten   a raise?

B.   Yes,   she has.
     She got   a raise   last May.

buy	dance	fly	go	read	see	swim
clean	eat	give	make	ride	study	take

1. A. What's the matter, Susan? You aren't riding very well today.

   B. I know. _____I haven't ridden_____ in a long time.

2. A. I can't believe it! These cars are very expensive.

   B. Remember, we _____ a new car in a long time.

3. A. Are you nervous?

   B. Yes, I am. _____ in an airplane in a long time.

4. A. Are you excited about your vacation?

   B. Yes, I am. _____ a vacation in a long time.

5. A. You aren't swimming very well today.

   B. I know. _____ in a long time.

6. A. Buster is really hungry.

   B. I know. He _____ anything in a long time.

7. A. Susie's room is very dirty.

   B. I know. She _____ it in a long time.

8. A. I think Timmy watches too much TV.

   B. You're right. _____ a book in a long time.

9. A. Mom, who was the sixteenth president of the United States?

B. I'm not sure. _____ American history in a long time.

10. A. Everyone says the new movie at the Center Cinema is excellent.

B. Let's see it. We _____ a good movie in a long time.

11. A. Are you nervous?

B. Yes, I am. _____ blood in a long time.

12. A. What's Dad doing?

B. He's making dinner. _____ dinner in a long time.

13. A. Is there any fruit in the refrigerator?

B. No, there isn't. I _____ to the supermarket in a long time.

14. A. Ouch!!

B. Sorry. _____ in a long time.

M **PUZZLE:** *What Have They Already Done?*

Across

1. wash
5. fly
8. go
10. explain
11. meet
12. take

Down

2. see
3. drive
4. play
6. wear
7. drink
8. get
9. be

Crossword puzzle with 1 across filled in: WASHED

Richard is going to have
a party tonight, and he has
a lot of things to do.

✔	go to the supermarket
	clean my apartment
✔	get a haircut
	bake a cake
✔	fix my CD player

1. _____ He's already gone to the supermarket. _____
2. _____ He hasn't cleaned his apartment yet. _____
3. _____
4. _____
5. _____

Susan is going to work this
morning, and she has a lot
of things to do.

✔	take a shower
	do my exercises
	feed the cat
✔	walk the dog
	eat breakfast

6. _____
7. _____
8. _____
9. _____
10. _____

Beverly and Paul are going on
a trip tomorrow, and they
have a lot of things to do.

	do our laundry
✔	get our paychecks
✔	pay our bills
	pack our suitcases
	say good-bye to our friends

11. _____
12. _____
13. _____
14. _____
15. _____

Roberta is very busy today.
She has a lot of things to
do at the office.

write to Mrs. Lane	✔
call Mr. Sanchez	✔
meet with Ms. Wong	
read my e-mail	
send a fax to the Ace Company	✔

16. _____

17. _____

18. _____

19. _____

20. _____

You have a lot of things to do today. What have you done? What haven't you done?

1. ....

2. ....

3. ....

4. ....

5. ....

○ **LISTENING**

What things have these people done? What haven't they done? Listen and check *Yes* or *No*.

		Yes	No			Yes	No
1.	do homework	✔		5.	do the laundry		✔
	practice the violin		✔		vacuum the rugs		✔
2.	write the report		✔	6.	get the food	✔	
	send a fax		✔		clean the house	✔	
3.	feed the dog	✔		7.	speak to the landlord	✔	
	eat breakfast		✔		call Ajax Electric	✔	✔
4.	fix the pipes	✔		8.	hook up the VCR	✔	
	repair the washing machine	✔			read the instructions	✔	✔

P WHAT ARE THEY SAYING?

1. A. Have you spoken to David recently?

   B. Yes, I __have__. I _____ to him last night.

   A. What _____ he say?

   B. He's worried because he's going to fly in a helicopter

      this week, and he's never _____ in a
      helicopter before.

2. A. _____ you seen any good movies recently?

   B. No, I _____. I _____ a movie last week,
      but it was terrible.

   A. Really? What movie did you _____?

   B. *The Man from Madagascar.* It's one of the worst

      movies I've ever _____.

3. A. I think I forgot to do something, but I can't remember
      what I forgot to do.

   B. Have you _____ the mail to the post office?

   A. Yes. I _____ it to the post office an hour ago.

   B. _____ you _____ a fax to the Ace Company?

   A. Yes. I _____ them a fax this morning.

   B. _____ you _____ the employees their
      paychecks?

   A. Uh-oh! That's what I forgot to do!

4. A. _____ you gone on vacation yet?

   B. Yes, I _____. I _____ to Venice.
      It was phenomenal!

   A. _____ you ever _____ to Venice before?

   B. Yes, I _____. I _____ there a few years
      ago.

5. A. What _____ you get for your birthday?

B. My family _____ me seventy-five dollars.

A. That's fantastic! What _____?

B. Going to buy? I've already _____ all my birthday money.

A. Really? What _____ buy?

B. I _____ a lot of CDs. Do you want to _____ to them?

6. A. Are you ready to leave soon?

B. No, _____. I haven't _____ a shower yet.

A. But you _____ up an hour ago. You're really slow today. _____ you eaten breakfast yet?

B. Of course _____. I _____ a little while ago, and I've already _____ the dishes.

A. Well, hurry up! It's 8:30. I don't want to be late.

Q LISTENING

Listen to each word and then say it.

1. job	10. you
2. jacket	11. yoga
3. juice	12. yellow
4. jam	13. yard
5. jog	14. yesterday
6. pajamas	15. young
7. journalist	16. yogurt
8. just	17. yet
9. Jennifer	18. New York

JULIA'S BROKEN KEYBOARD

Julia's keyboard is broken. The j's and the y's don't always work.
Fill in the missing j's and y's and then read Julia's letters aloud.

1.

_J_udy,

   Have you seen my blue and
_y_ellow _j_acket at ___our house?
I think I left it there ___esterday
after the ___azz concert. I've looked
everywhere, and I ___ust can't find
it anywhere.

                              ___ulia

2.

Dear ___ennifer,

   We're sorry ___ou haven't been able
to visit us this ___ear. Do ___ou think
___ou could come in ___une or ___uly?
We really en___oyed ___our visit last
___ear. We really want to see ___ou
again.

                              ___ulia

3.

___eff,

   ___ack and I have gone out ___ogging,
but we'll be back in ___ust a few
minutes. Make ___ourself comfortable.
___ou can wait for us in the ___ard. We
haven't eaten lunch ___et. We'll have
some ___ogurt and orange ___uice when
we get back.

                              ___ulia

4.

Dear ___ane,

   We ___ust received the beautiful
pa___amas ___ou sent to ___immy.
Thank ___ou very much. ___immy is
too ___oung to write to ___ou himself,
but he says "Thank ___ou." He's
already worn the pa___amas, and
he's en___oying them a lot.

                              ___ulia

5.

Dear ___anet,

   ___ack and I are coming to visit
___ou and ___ohn in New ___ork. We've
been to New ___ork before, but we
haven't visited the Statue of Liberty
or the Empire State Building ___et.
See ___ou in ___anuary or maybe in
___une.

                              ___ulia

6.

Dear ___oe,

   We got a letter from ___ames last
week. He has en___oyed college a lot
this ___ear. His favorite sub___ects
are German and ___apanese. He's
looking for a ___ob as a ___ournalist
in ___apan, but he hasn't found one
___et.

                              ___ulia

IS OR HAS?

1. He's already eaten lunch.

   _____ is

   __✔__ has

2. He's eating lunch.

   __✔__ is

   _____ has

3. She's taking a bath.

   _____ is

   _____ has

4. She's taken a bath.

   _____ is

   _____ has

5. He's having a good time.

   _____ is

   _____ has

6. She's going to get up.

   _____ is

   _____ has

7. He's bought a lot of CDs recently.

   _____ is

   _____ has

8. It's snowing.

   _____ is

   _____ has

9. She's thirsty.

   _____ is

   _____ has

10. He's got to leave now.

    _____ is

    _____ has

11. Where's the nearest health club?

    _____ is

    _____ has

12. She's written the report.

    _____ is

    _____ has

13. He's taking a lot of photographs.

    _____ is

    _____ has

14. He's taken a few photographs.

    _____ is

    _____ has

15. He's spent all his money.

    _____ is

    _____ has

16. There's a library across the street.

    _____ is

    _____ has

17. She's gone kayaking.

    _____ is

    _____ has

18. It's very warm.

    _____ is

    _____ has

19. He's embarrassed.

    _____ is

    _____ has

20. This is the best book she's ever read.

    _____ is

    _____ has

A HOW LONG?

for	since

1. *How long have you had a headache?*

   I've had a headache
   __since__ this morning.

2. How long have your parents been married?

   _____ a long time.

3. How long has your brother owned a motorcycle?

   _____ last summer.

4. How long has your sister been interested in astronomy?

   _____ several years.

5. How long have you had a cell phone?

   _____ last month.

6. How long have you and your husband known each other?

   _____ 1994.

7. How long have the Wilsons had a dog?

   _____ a few weeks.

8. How long have you had problems with your upstairs neighbor?

   _____ a year.

9. How long has your daughter been a computer programmer?

   _____ 2000.

10. How long has your son played in the school orchestra?

    _____ September.

11. How long have there been mice in your attic?

    _____ two months.

B WHAT'S THE QUESTION?

1. _____How long has_____ your daughter _____wanted to be an engineer_____?

   She's wanted to be an engineer for a long time.

2. _____ James _____?

   He's owned his own house since 2001.

3. _____ your grandparents _____?

   They've been married for 50 years.

4. _____ you _____?

   I've been interested in photography since last year.

5. _____ Gregory _____?

   He's worn glasses since last spring.

6. _____ your cousins _____?

   They've known how to snowboard for a few years.

7. _____ your son _____?

   He's had a girlfriend for several months.

8. _____ there _____?

   There's been a pizza shop in town since last fall.

Listen. Then clap and practice.

A. How long have you   known   Maria?

B. I've known her   since I was   two.

A. Have you met   her older   sister?

B. No, I haven't.   Have you?

A. How long   has your son   been in college?

B. He's been there   since early   September.

A. Does he like   all of his   courses?

B. I think so.   I can't   remember.

A. How long have   your friends   lived in London?

B. They've lived there   since two thousand   one.

A. Have you visited them   since they   moved there?

B. Yes, I have.   It was fun.

A. How long has   your brother   been married?

B. He's been married   for seven   months.

A. Have you seen him   since   his wedding?

B. I've seen him   only   once.

D SINCE WHEN?

1. _____I'm_____ sick today.

   _____I've been sick_____ since I got up this morning.

3. Roger _____ how to ski.

   _____ how to ski since he took lessons last winter.

5. _____we're_____ lost.

   _____we've been_____ lost since we arrived here this morning.

7. _____It's_____ cold and cloudy.

   _____It has been_____ cold and cloudy since we got here last weekend.

9. My boyfriend _____has_____ bored.

   _____he's been_____ bored since the concert began forty-five minutes ago.

2. Rita _____ a swollen knee.

   _____ a swollen knee since she played soccer last Saturday.

4. _____ nervous.

   _____ nervous since they got married a few hours ago.

6. I _____have_____ a stiff neck.

   _____I've had_____ a stiff neck since I went to a tennis match yesterday.

8. My daughter _____plays_____ the cello.

   _____She's_____ played the cello since she was six years old.

10. _____I'm_____ afraid of dogs.

   _____I've been_____ afraid of dogs since my neighbor's dog bit me last year.

Activity Workbook   55

E LISTENING

Listen and choose the correct answer.

1. a. Bob is in the army.
   b. Bob is engaged.

2. a. Carol is in music school.
   b. Carol is a professional musician.

3. **a.** Michael has been home for a week.
   b. Michael hurt himself this week.

4. a. She hasn't started her new job.
   b. She gets up early every morning.

5. **a.** Richard is in college.
   b. Richard hasn't eaten in the cafeteria.

6. **a.** Nancy and Tom met five and a half years ago.
   b. Nancy and Tom met when they were five and a half years old.

7. **a.** They play soccer every weekend.
   b. They're eight years old.

8. a. Patty is a teenager.
   b. Patty has short hair.

9. a. Ron used to own his own business.
   b. Ron moved nine years ago.

10. **a.** She's interested in astronomy.
    b. She's eleven years old.

11. a. He's in high school.
    b. He isn't in high school now.

12. **a.** Alan has owned his house for fifteen years.
    b. Alan doesn't have problems with his house now.

F CROSSWORD

| dizzy | fever | measles | nauseous | sore | stiff |

Across

3. My throat has been very _____ since Tuesday.
4. I haven't been able to eat since yesterday. I feel _nauseous_.
6. I've had a _____ neck for a week.

Down

1. I've had a high _fever_ for 24 hours.
2. My children have had little red spots all over their bodies for two days. They have the _measles_.
5. I've been _dizzy_ since I fell down and hurt my head.

56   **Activity Workbook**

G SCRAMBLED SENTENCES

Unscramble the sentences.

1. she   a   jazz   Julie   liked   teenager.   has   was   since

   Julie has liked jazz since she was a teenager.

2. he   play   little   the   since   known   a   boy.   He's   piano   was   how   to

   He's known how to play the piano since he was a little

3. since   I've   was   in   I   astronomy   young.   interested   been

   I've been interested in astronomy since I was young

4. since   been   they   college.   engaged   They've   finished

   They've been

5. been   he   a   cooking   He's   graduated   from   chef   school.   since

   _____

6. she   wanted   be   to   teacher   eighteen   She's   a   years   since   old.   was

   _____

7. moved   ago.   business   They've   their   year   owned   since   a   they   here   own

   _____

H WRITE ABOUT YOURSELF

1. I'm interested in _____.

   I've been interested in _____ since _____.

2. I own _____.

   I've owned _____ since _____.

3. I like _____.

   I've _____ since _____.

4. I want to _____.

   I've _____ since _____.

5. I know how to _____.

   I've _____ since _____.

be	have	speak	teach	visit	walk

Pahk the cah!

1. Mr. and Mrs. Miller ___walk___ every day.

    _____ every day since Mr.
    Miller had problems with his heart last

    year. Before that, _____ never

    _____. They stayed home and
    watched TV.

2. Sam _____ with a Boston accent.

    _____ with a Boston accent
    since he moved to Boston last summer.

    Before that, _____ with a New
    York accent.

NATIONAL
TRUCKING

3. Terry _____ a truck driver. She
    drives a truck between the east coast

    and the west coast. _____
    a truck driver for a year. Before that,

    _____ a taxi driver.

4. Before he moved to Brazil, Professor Baker

    _____ French. Now _____

    English. _____ English
    at a Brazilian university for the past two
    years.

5. Your Uncle Walter _____ already

    _____ us five times this year!

    Last year, he _____ us only
    twice. How many times will he

    _____ us next year?!

6. Tiffany _____ long blonde hair.

    _____ long blonde hair since she
    became a movie star. Before that, she

    _____ short brown hair. Tiffany looks
    very different now!

Victor
(be)

musician	1990–now
photographer	1982–1989

Mrs. Sanchez
(teach)

science	1995–now
math	1985–1994

my grandparents
(have)

dog	1998–now
cat	1986–1997

Betty
(work)

bank	2000–now
mall	1997–1999

my parents
(live)

Miami	2001–now
New York	1980–2000

1. How long _____*has Victor been*_____ a musician?

   _____*He's been a musician*_____ since ____*1990*____.

2. How long _____*was he*_____ a photographer?

   _____*He was a photographer*_____ for ____*7 years*____.

3. How long _____ science?

   _____ since _____.

4. How long _____ math?

   _____ for _____.

5. How long __*have you grandparent had*__ a cat?

   they've had a cat for __*11 years*__.

6. How long __*have they had*__ a dog?

   they've had a dog since __*1998*__.

7. How long _____ at the bank?

   _____ since _____.

8. How long _____ at the mall?

   _____ for _____.

9. How long _____ in New York?

   _____ for _____.

10. How long _____ in Miami?

    _____ since _____.

REUNION

1. Do you still go skiing every winter?

No. ....
.... (for/since) ....
....

2. Do you still live .... ?

No. ....
.... (for/since) ....
....

3. Are you still a/an .... ?

No. ....
.... (for/since) ....
....

4. How long have you been interested in .... ?

....
.... (for/since) ....
....

5. Do you still .... in your free time?

No. ....
.... (for/since) ....
....

6. Do your brothers still call you "Tiny Tim"?

No. _____
_____ (for/since) _____.

7. How long have you _____ ?

_____
_____ (for/since) _____.

8. Do you still _____ ?

No. _____
_____ (for/since) _____.

L LISTENING

Listen and choose the correct answer.

1. a. He's always been a salesperson.
    b. He was a cashier.

2. a. His daughter was in medical school.
    b. His daughter is in medical school.

3. a. Her parents haven't always lived in a house.
    b. Her parents have always lived in a house.

4. a. He's always wanted to be an actor.
    b. He isn't in college now.

5. a. They exercise at their health club every day.
    b. They haven't exercised at their health club since last year.

6. a. James hasn't always been a bachelor.
    b. James has been married for ten years.

7. a. Jane has wanted to meet a writer.
    b. Jane wants to be a writer.

8. a. He's never broken his ankle.
    b. He's never sprained his ankle.

9. a. She's always liked rock music.
    b. She hasn't always liked classical music.

10. a. Billy has had a fever for two days.
    b. Billy has had a sore throat for two days.

11. a. Jennifer has always been the manager.
    b. Jennifer hasn't been a salesperson since last fall.

12. a. He's interested in modern art now.
    b. He's always been interested in art.

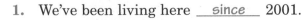

for	since

1. We've been living here ___since___ 2001.

2. It's been raining _____ two days.

3. I've been listening to this CD _____ an hour.

4. She's been flying airplanes _____ 1995.

5. Billy, you've been roller-blading _____ this morning!

6. He's been practicing the cello _____ three and a half hours.

7. Our neighbors have been vacuuming

_____ 7 A.M.

8. We've been having problems with our

heat _____ a week.

B **CHOOSE**

1. I've been working here since _____.
   a. last month
   b. three months

2. He's been taking a shower for _____.
   a. this afternoon
   b. half an hour

3. It's been ringing for _____.
   a. two o'clock
   b. a few minutes

4. She's been studying since _____.
   a. eight o'clock
   b. an hour

5. They've been dating for _____.
   a. high school
   b. six months

6. I've been feeling sick since _____.
   a. twelve hours
   b. yesterday

C HOW LONG?

1. How long have you been studying?

<u>I've been studying since</u>

early this morning.

2. How long has Ann been feeling sick?

_____

a few days.

3. How long has Tom been having problems with his car?

_____

a week.

4. How long have the people next door been arguing?

_____

last night.

5. How long have we been waiting?

_____

forty-five minutes.

6. How long has that cell phone been ringing?

_____

the play began.

7. How long has Professor Drake been talking?

_____

an hour and a half.

8. How long have Rick and Sally been dating?

_____

high school.

9. How long have you been teaching?

_____

1975.

10. How long have I been chatting online?

_____

more than two hours.

D WHAT ARE THEY DOING?

assemble	bake	bark	browse	do	jog	look	make	plant

1. Larry ____is looking____ for his keys.

   ____He's been looking____ for his keys all morning.

2. My sister _____ in the park.

   _____ in the park since 8 A.M.

3. The dog next door _____.

   _____ all day.

4. Our neighbors _____ flowers.

   _____ flowers for several hours.

5. Michael _____ his homework.

   _____ his homework since dinner.

6. My wife _____ the web.

   _____ the web for an hour.

7. Mr. and Mrs. Lee _____ their son's new bicycle.

   _____ it all afternoon.

8. I'm _____ cookies.

   _____ cookies since two o'clock.

9. You and your brother _____ a lot of noise!

   _____ noise since you got up.

E LISTENING

Listen and choose the correct time expressions to complete the sentences.

1. a. 1995. *(a circled)*
   b. a few years.

2. a. 1:45.
   b. forty-five minutes.

3. a. 3 o'clock.
   b. thirty minutes.

4. a. yesterday.
   b. several days.

5. a. 7:30 this morning.
   b. more than an hour.

6. a. 7 o'clock.
   b. a half hour.

7. a. a few weeks.
   b. last month.

8. a. about three hours.
   b. 4 o'clock.

9. a. early this morning.
   b. twenty minutes.

F GRAMMARRAP: *How Long?*

Listen. Then clap and practice.

A.   How long have you been   working   at the mall?

B.   I've been working   at the mall   since the fall.

A.   How long has she been   wearing   her new ring?

B.   She's been wearing   her new ring   since the spring.

A.   How long have you been   living   in L.A.?

B.   We've been living   in L.A.   since May.

A.   How long has he been   waiting   for the train?

B.   He's been waiting   since it started   to rain.

A.   How long have you been   looking for   that mouse?

B.   We've been looking   since we rented   this house.

WHAT ARE THEY SAYING?

make	play	run	snow	study	take	vacuum	wait	wear	work

1. Excuse me. _Have you been waiting_ in line for a long time?

   Yes, I ___have___. _I've been waiting_ for more than an hour.

2. What a terrible day! _____ for a long time?

   Yes, _____. since early this morning.

3. Your son plays the violin very beautifully. _____ lessons for a long time?

   Yes, _____. lessons since he was five.

4. _____ here for a long time?

   No, _____. I've _____ here for only a week.

5. _____ your car _____ strange noises for a long time?

   Yes, _____. these noises all week.

6. You look tired. _____ for a long time?

   Yes, _____. all morning.

7. Your children speak French very well.

_____ it for a long time?

Yes, _____.

_____ French for six years.

8. I'm really tired.

_____ for a long time?

Yes, we _____.

_____ since 6 A.M.

9. Your pants are dirty.

_____ them all week?

No, _____.

_____ them for only a few hours.

10. This is the sixth game you've won today.

_____ for a long time?

No, _____.

_____ for only a few months.

H LISTENING

Listen and choose what the people are talking about.

1. a. traffic
    b. a computer

2. a. a wall
    b. the furniture

3. a. the guitar
    b. my bills

4. a. the drums
    b. tennis

5. a. the cookies
    b. the babies

6. a. the cake
    b. the bridge

7. a. her composition
    b. her bicycle

8. a. books
    b. trains

9. a. a sandwich
    b. a novel

10. a. socks
    b. chairs

11. a. the president
    b. CDs

12. a. a restaurant
    b. a neighbor

13. a. fruit
    b. my car

14. a. a test
    b. a cake

15. a. videos
    b. problems

SOUND IT OUT!

Listen to each word and then say it.

this

1.	b<u>i</u>lls	3.	ch<u>i</u>cken	5.	b<u>ui</u>lding	
2.	off<u>i</u>cer	4.	t<u>i</u>cket	6.	<u>i</u>tself	

these

1.	w<u>ee</u>k	3.	bri<u>e</u>fcase	5.	f<u>e</u>ver	
2.	sp<u>ea</u>k	4.	friendl<u>y</u>	6.	<u>ea</u>ten	

Listen and put a circle around the word that has the same sound.

1. th<u>i</u>n: pol<u>i</u>ce   t<u>i</u>red   (<u>i</u>nterested)

2. b<u>ui</u>ld: h<u>ea</u>dache   (<u>i</u>s)   sw<u>ea</u>ter

3. r<u>ea</u>d: (St<u>e</u>ve's)   b<u>ee</u>n   tr<u>y</u>

4. <u>i</u>f: (<u>i</u>n)   b<u>i</u>te   tax<u>i</u>

5. l<u>i</u>ve: m<u>e</u>t   (h<u>i</u>story)   ch<u>i</u>ld

6. f<u>i</u>shing: sc<u>i</u>ence   wr<u>i</u>ting   (s<u>i</u>ster)

7. p<u>ie</u>ce: ver<u>y</u>   w<u>ea</u>r   (w<u>i</u>nter)

8. <u>ea</u>st: h<u>i</u>re   (Ch<u>i</u>nese)   r<u>ea</u>dy

Now make a sentence using all the words you circled, and read the sentence aloud.

9. ....

10. k<u>ey</u>:   d<u>i</u>nner   (rec<u>ei</u>ve)   th<u>i</u>nk

11. tenn<u>i</u>s: <u>ea</u>sy   h<u>ea</u>ter   (th<u>i</u>s)

12. compl<u>e</u>te: (<u>a</u>ny)   g<u>e</u>t   tr<u>y</u>

13. k<u>ee</u>p: b<u>u</u>sy   (P<u>e</u>ter)   d<u>i</u>sturb

14. tux<u>e</u>do: t<u>y</u>pe   <u>i</u>f   (w<u>ee</u>k)

15. L<u>i</u>nda: (d<u>i</u>dn't)   gr<u>ee</u>n   br<u>i</u>ght

16. m<u>ee</u>ting: ch<u>i</u>ld   forg<u>e</u>t   (<u>e</u>-mail)

Now make a sentence using all the words you circled, and read the sentence aloud.

17. ....

J YOU DECIDE: *What Have They Been Doing?*

1. I have a sore throat.

No wonder you have a sore throat!

You've been singing all day.

2. My back hurts.

No wonder your back hurts!

_____ all day.

3. Bob has a terrible sunburn.

No wonder he has a terrible sunburn!

_____ all day.

4. Nancy is very tired.

No wonder she's very tired!

_____ all day.

5. Jane and I have headaches.

No wonder you have headaches!

_____ all day.

6. Bob and Judy are very disappointed.

No wonder they're very disappointed!

_____ all day.

7. I can't finish my dinner.

No wonder you can't finish your dinner!

_____ all day.

8. Victor doesn't have any money.

No wonder he doesn't have any money!

_____ all day.

| complain | eat | go | make | read | see | study | swim | talk | write |

1. My husband and I are very full. ___We've been eating___ for the past two hours. __We've__ already ___eaten___ soup, salad, chicken, and vegetables. And our dinner isn't finished. ___We haven't eaten___ our dessert yet!

2. Dr. Davis is tired. _____ *seeing* patients since early this morning. _____ already _____ twenty patients, and it's only two o'clock. _____ the other patients in her waiting room yet.

3. Dave likes to swim. _____ for an hour and a half. _____ already _____ across the pool thirty times.

4. Amy is very tired. _____ to job interviews for the past three weeks. _____ already _____ to ten job interviews, and she hasn't found a job yet!

5. Gregory loves to talk. _____ all evening. _____ already _____ about his job, his house, and his car. Fortunately, _____ about his cats yet.

6. Betty and Bob are writing thank-you notes for their wedding gifts, and they're very tired. _____ them all weekend. _____ already _____ to their aunts, uncles, and cousins, but _____ to their friends yet.

7. Andrew is tired. He's having a party tonight, and _____

_____ desserts since early this morning.

_____ already _____ two apple pies and three

blueberry pies. But he isn't finished. _he hasn't made_

a chocolate cake yet.

8. Patty is very tired. _____ since she got home

from school. _____ already _____ English and math.

And she'll be up late tonight because _____
for her history test yet.

9. Today is Howard's day off, and he's enjoying himself. _____

_____ since early this morning. _____ already

_____ three short stories. But _____

today's newspaper yet.

10. Mr. and Mrs. Grumble like to complain. _____

all evening. _____ already _____ about their jobs; the
weather, and several members of their family. Fortunately, they

_____ about the party yet, but I'm sure they will.

L LISTENING

Listen and decide where the conversation is taking place.

1. (a.) in a kitchen
   b. in a supermarket

2. a. at home
   (b.) in school

3. a. in a department store
   (b.) in a laundromat

4. (a.) at a movie theater
   b. at home

5. (a.) at a clinic
   b. at a bakery

6. a. in a cafeteria
   (b.) in a library

7. a. at a concert hall
   (b.) at a museum

8. (a.) at a health club
   b. in a book store

9. a. in an office
   (b.) at a bus stop

10. a. at a zoo
    (b.) in a pet shop

11. (a.) at home
    b. at a movie theater

12. a. at a clinic
    (b.) in a department store

1. The floor is wet! How long has the ceiling been [(leaking) / leaked] ?

2. I'm not nervous. I've been [flown / flying] in helicopters for years.

3. I'm a little worried. I've never [been running / run] in a marathon before.

4. How many pizzas have you already [made / been making] so far today?

5. You look tired. What [have you / have you been] doing today?

6. I think I've [seen / been seeing] this movie before.

7. Has your husband already [giving / given] blood?

8. I've never [taken / been taking] a karate lesson. Have you?

9. Have you ever [been going / gone] out on a date before?

10. Alexander, your cell phone [has rung / has been ringing] since we started class!

11. Jane isn't nervous. She's been [sung / singing] in front of audiences for years.

N YOU DECIDE: *What Are They Saying?*

A. Mrs. Vickers, could I speak to you for a few minutes?

B. Of course. Please sit down.

A. Mrs. Vickers, I've been thinking. I've been working here at the

.... Company (for/since) ....
I've worked very hard, and I've done a lot of things here.

For example, I've .... ,

I've .... ,

and I've been ....

(for/since) ....

B. That's true, Mr. Mills. And we're happy with your work.

A. Thank you, Mrs. Vickers. As I was saying, I know I've done a
very good job here, and I really think I should get a raise.

I haven't had a raise (for/since) ....

B. ....

A. ....

A. Dad, could I speak to you for a few minutes?

B. Sure, James. Please sit down.

A. Dad, I've been thinking. I've been working very hard in school
this year, and I've done all my chores at home. For example,

I've .... , I've ....

.... , and I've been ....

.... (for/since) ....

B. That's true, James. Your mother and I are very proud of you.

A. Thank you, Dad. As I was saying, I know I've been very
responsible, and I really think I should be able to take your
car when I go out on a date. After all, I've been driving

(for/since) ....

B. ....

A. ....

Daniel has been living in a small town in Mexico all his life. His father just got a good job in the United States, and Daniel and his family are going to live there. Daniel's life is going to be very different in the United States.

1.   He's going to live in a big city.
2.   He's going to take English lessons.
3.   He's going to take the subway.
4.   He's going to shop in American supermarkets.
5.   He's going to eat American food.
6.   He's going to play American football.

7.   He's going to _____.

Daniel is a little nervous.

1. _____ He's never lived in a big city _____ before.

2. _____ before.

3. _____ before.

4. _____ before.

5. _____ before.

6. _____ before.

7. _____ before.

Daniel's cousins have been living in the United States for many years. They'll be able to help him.

8. _____ They've been living in a big city _____ for years.

9. _____ for years.

10. _____ for years.

11. _____ for years.

12. _____ for years.

13. _____ for years.

14. _____ for years.

Daniel's cousins tell him he shouldn't worry. They're sure he'll enjoy his new life in the United States very much.

YOU DECIDE: *A New Life*

_____ has been living in _____

all her life. Now she's going to move to _____ .
                                                    (your city)

Her life is going to be very different in _____ .
                                                    (your city)

1. She's going to _____ .

2. She's going to _____ .

3. She's going to _____ .

4. She's going to _____ .

5. She's going to _____ .

_____ is a little nervous.

6. _____ before.

7. _____ before.

8. _____ before.

9. _____ before.

10. _____ before.

_____ (has/have) been living in _____ for many
years and will be able to help her.

11. _____ for years.

12. _____ for years.

13. _____ for years.

14. _____ for years.

15. _____ for years.

_____ shouldn't worry. I'm sure she'll enjoy her new life in _____
very much.

A.   Complete the sentences with the present perfect.

Ex. *(do)*   Julie __has__ already __done__ her homework.

     (read)   I ____haven't read____ your report yet.

(eat)   **1.** Mary and her brother _____ already _____ breakfast.

(take)   **2.** My nephew _____ his violin lesson yet.

(write)   **3.** I _____ to my grandparents yet.

(go)   **4.** My wife _____ already _____ to work.

(pay)   **5.** You _____ your electric bill yet.

(have)   **6.** Henry _____ already _____ a problem with his new cell phone.

B.   Complete the questions.

1. A. __have you spoken__ to your
         supervisor yet?

   B. Yes, I have. I spoke to her this morning.

2. A. __has he ridden__ his new bicycle
         yet?

   B. Yes, he has. He rode it this morning.

3. A. __have they gotten__ their paychecks
         yet?

   B. Yes, they have. They got them this
         afternoon.

4. A. __has he__ ever __flown__
         in a helicopter?

   B. Yes, he has. He flew in a helicopter
         last summer.

5. A. __has she__ ever __been__ on TV?

   B. Yes, she has. She was on TV last week.

6. A. __have you met__ your daughter's
         new boyfriend yet?

   B. No, I haven't. I'm going to meet him
         tonight.

C.   Complete the sentences.

Ex. My neck is very stiff. _____It's been_____ stiff since I got up this morning.

     Tom is reading his e-mail. ____He's been reading____ it for a half hour.

1. It's sunny. _____ all week.

2. We're browsing the web. ____browsing_____ the web since 8 o'clock.

3. My daughter has a fever. ____had_____ a fever since early this morning.

4. My son is studying. ____studying_____ since he got home from school.

5. Our neighbors are arguing. ____arguing_____ all afternoon.

6. I know how to skate. ____I've known_____ how to skate since I was six years old.

7. Susan is interested in science. _She's been_ interested in science since she was a teenager.

8. My husband and I are cleaning our basement. _I've been cleaning_ it all weekend.

D. Complete the answers.

for	since

1. How long has your wife been working at the bank?

   _____ _since_ 1999.

2. How long have those dogs been barking?

   _____ a long time.

3. How long has it been snowing?

   _____ two days.

4. How long have you wanted to be an astronaut?

   _____ I was six years old.

E. Complete the sentences.

1. My brother owns a motorcycle. _he's owned_ a motorcycle since last summer.

   Before that, _he owned_ a bicycle.

2. I'm a journalist. _I've been_ a journalist since 2000.

   Before that, _I was_ an actor.

3. My daughter likes classical music. _____ classical music since she finished college.

   Before that, _____ rock music.

F. Listen and choose the correct answer.

1. a. Janet is in acting school.
   b. Janet is an actress.

2. a. The president has finished his speech.
   b. The president is still speaking.

3. a. They've been living in New York since 1995.
   b. They haven't lived in New York since 1995.

4. a. They're going to eat later.
   b. They're going to eat now.

5. a. She's called the superintendent.
   b. She has to call the superintendent.

6. a. Someone is helping Billy with his homework.
   b. No one is helping Billy with his homework.

A WHAT DO THEY { ENJOY DOING / LIKE TO DO } ?

| enjoy _____ing | like to _____ | _____ing |

1. My wife and I _____enjoy_____ relaxing on the beach when we go on vacation.

2. Mrs. Finn is very talkative. She _____likes to_____ talk about her grandchildren.

    _____Talking_____ about her grandchildren is important to her.

3. Billy doesn't _____enjoy_____ going to the doctor, but he went yesterday for his annual checkup.

4. I _____like to_____ knit sweaters. _____knitting_____ sweaters is a good way to relax.

5. My husband doesn't _____enjoy_____ asking for a raise, but sometimes he has to.

6. Dr. Brown _____likes to_____ deliver babies. In her opinion, _____delivering_____ babies is the best job in the world.

7. Bob doesn't _____enjoy_____ being a bachelor. He thinks _____being_____ married is better.

8. Ann _____likes to_____ plant flowers. She thinks _____planting_____ flowers is good exercise.

9. Jim _____enjoys_____ chatting online with his friends, but his parents think _____chatting_____ online every evening isn't a very good idea.

10. Tom doesn't _____like to_____ play hockey. He thinks _____playing_____ hockey is dangerous.

11. My parents go to the gym during the winter, but in the summer they _____enjoy_____ going hiking.

12. Martin _____likes to_____ go to parties. He thinks _____going_____ to parties is a good way to meet people.

13. I really want to play the piano well, but I don't _____enjoy_____ practicing.

78   Activity Workbook

B GRAMMARRAP: *Writing Is Fun*

Listen. Then clap and practice.

Writing is fun.
I like to write.
I enjoy writing letters late at night.

Eating is fun.
I like to eat.
I enjoy eating fish, and I like eating meat.

Skiing is great.
He likes to ski.
But skiing's been hard since he hurt his knee.

Singing is fun.
She likes to sing.
But today she's sick, and she can't sing a thing.

Running is great.
They like to run.
Swimming's okay, but running's more fun.

Baking is great.
He likes to bake.
When he's feeling sad, he bakes a cake.

Knitting is fun.
She likes to knit.
She enjoys knitting sweaters, but none of them fit!

Activity Workbook 79

WHAT'S THE WORD?

clean	complain	eat	go	sit	wear
cleaning	complaining	eating	going	sitting	wearing

1. I hate to _____complain_____, but your loud music is disturbing me.

2. Carol tries to avoid _____Sitting_____ in the sun.

3. Sally likes to _____eat_____ dinner at home.

4. My son hates to _____clean_____ his room.

5. Richard can't stand to _____wear_____ a tie.

6. Tom avoids _____cleaning_____ his apartment whenever he can.

7. James doesn't like to _____go_____ to the mall.

8. My husband and I hate _____going_____ sailing.

9. My wife and I like to _____sit_____ in the park on a sunny day.

10. Please try to avoid _____complaining_____ about the weather all the time.

11. My friends and I can't stand _____eating_____ in fast-food restaurants.

12. My daughter likes _____wearing_____ the sweater you gave her for her birthday.

D **GRAMMARRAP:** *Pet Peeves*

Listen. Then clap and practice.

I don't like	waiting	for the bus	in the rain.
I hate to	rush	when I'm late	for a plane.
I avoid	talking	to strangers	on the train.
I can't stand	driving	in the center	lane.

I don't like to	iron	on a hot	summer day.
I hate to clean	the house	in the middle	of May.
I avoid	dusting	and sweeping	my floors.
I can't stand	doing	all my household	chores!

E YOU DECIDE: *What's the Reason?*

1. David is happy he works in a gym because he enjoys

   exercising every day.

2. Gloria hates being a taxi driver because she can't stand

   driving.

3. Miguel is glad he lives in Puerto Rico because he likes

   speaking spanish.

4. I'm sorry I'm a secretary because I can't stand

   teaching.

5. We're happy we're going camping because we enjoy

   going to the beach.

6. William is upset he's sick because he hates

   staying at home.

7. I'm glad I have a new bicycle because I like

   riding.

8. Norman doesn't like being on a diet because he can't stand

   eating Jonk food.

9. Julie is happy she's a Hollywood actress because she enjoys

   acting.

F MY ENERGETIC GRANDFATHER

A. Your grandfather is very energetic!

B. He sure is!

A. When did he start _playing_ ¹ the drums?

B. Believe it or not, he learned _to play_ ² the drums when he was sixty years old!

A. That's incredible! Does he _play_ ³ the drums often?

B. Yes, he does. He's played every day for the last eight years.

A. What else does he enjoy doing?

B. He enjoys _singing_ ⁴, he enjoys _chatting_ ⁵,

and he also enjoys _dancing_ ⁶.

A. I hope I have that much energy when I'm his age!

G I CAN'T STAND IT!

I spoke with my friend Pam last weekend, and she talked a lot about figure skating. Ever since she started to figure skate several months ago, that's all she ever talks about! I never go out with her anymore because she practices figure skating all the time. And whenever I talk to her on the phone, figure skating is the only thing she talks about! (She thinks that everybody should learn to figure skate.) I can't stand it! I don't ever want to hear another word about figure skating!

Now YOU tell about somebody.

I spoke to my friend _____ last weekend, and _____ talked a lot about

_____. Ever since _____

_____

_____

_____

_____

_____ .

CHOOSE

1. I've decided ~~buy~~ ~~buying~~ (to buy) a motorcycle.

2. Have you ever considered to move (moving) move ?

3. I'm thinking about (going) to go go on a diet.

4. You should consider to change change (changing) jobs.

5. Have you decided to (get) to get getting a dog?

6. He's thought about to retire (retiring) retire .

I **GRAMMARRAP:** *I Considered Ordering the Cheesecake*

Listen. Then clap and practice.

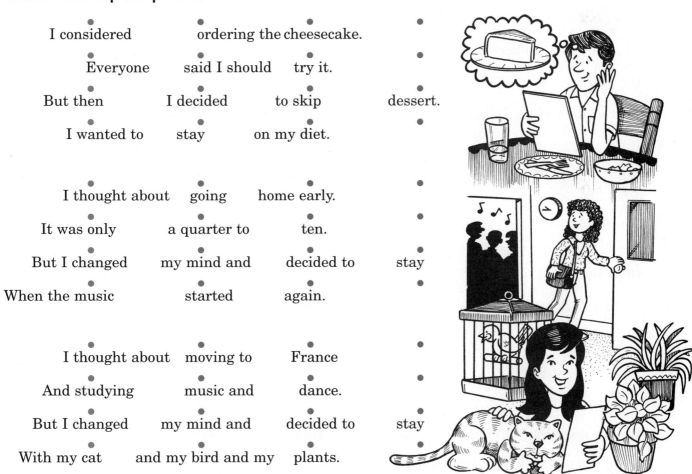

I considered   ordering the cheesecake.
     Everyone   said I should   try it.
But then   I decided   to skip   dessert.
     I wanted to   stay   on my diet.

     I thought about   going   home early.
It was only   a quarter to   ten.
But I changed   my mind and   decided to   stay
When the music   started   again.

     I thought about   moving to   France
And studying   music and   dance.
But I changed   my mind and   decided to   stay
With my cat   and my bird and my   plants.

Activity Workbook **83**

YOU DECIDE: *What's Carla Going to Do?*

A. Hi, Carla. How are you? We haven't spoken in a long time. Tell me, what have you been doing?

B. ....

A. Oh. And what are you thinking about doing after you finish studying English?

B. For a while, I considered .... ,

and then I thought about ....

But I finally decided to ....

A. Oh. Why did you decide to do that?

B. Because ....

A. That's interesting. Tell me, Carla, have you ever considered ....

.... ?

B. Yes. I thought about doing that, but decided it wasn't a very good idea.

A. Why not?

B. Because .... , ...

A. Oh, I see.

B. So, Kathy, do you think I'm making the right decision?

A. ....

B. Do you really think so?

A. ....

B. Well, it was great talking to you. Let's get together soon.

A. Okay. I'll call you and we'll make some plans.

K WHAT'S THE WORD?

1. You can't keep on ____rearranging____ the furniture so often. You rearranged it last weekend!

2. I stopped ____eating____ meat. I only eat fish and chicken.

3. He tried to quit ____worrying____, but he couldn't. He still worries about everything.

4. Alice always gets up late. She should start ____to get / getting____ up earlier.

5. Richard doesn't exercise very often. He should begin ____exercising / to exercise____ every day. He'll feel a lot better.

6. You can't continue ____ask / asking____ me the same question. You've already asked me ten times!

7. I realize that I can't keep on ____arguing____ with people. I'm never going to argue with anyone again!

8. I know that Dave takes piano lessons. When did he start ____to take / taking____ guitar lessons?

9. You should stop ____paying / to pay____ your bills late and start ____paying____ them on time.

10. Professor Blaine is very boring. Students continue ____to fall / falling____ asleep in his classes.

L GOOD DECISIONS

| bite | clean | cook | do | gossip | interrupt | make | pay |

This year I'm going to break all my bad habits. First, I've decided to stop ____biting____[1] my nails. I've also started ____to do / doing____[2] exercises every day. I learned ____to cook____[3] when I was young, so I've decided to start ____to cook / cooking____[4] healthy meals. I'm also considering ____paying____[5] my bills on time, and I'm thinking about ____cleaning____[6] my apartment every week. I've also decided to stop ____gossiping____[7] about other people and to stop ____interrupting____[8] my friends while they're talking.

1.  My husband can't stop _____falling_____ asleep at the movies. Every time we go, he falls asleep. If he keeps on ___falling___ asleep, I'll never go to a movie with him again.

2.  I don't think I should continue ___lifting/to___ weights every day. I like ___lifting/to___ weights, but I'm afraid I might hurt my back if I keep on ___lifting___ them so often.

3.  My older sister always teases me. Today I'm really mad! She began ___to tease___ me early this morning, and she hasn't stopped. If she keeps on ___teasing___ me, I'm going to cry. And I won't stop ___crying___ until she stops ___teasing___ me!

4.  My friend Albert has got to stop ___driving___ so fast and start ___driving to___ more carefully. If he continues ___driving___ fast, I'm sure he'll have a serious accident some day.

5.  Mr. Perkins, when are you going to stop ___dressing/to___ so sloppily and start ___dressing___ more neatly? If you keep on ___dressing___ like that, I'm going to have to fire you.

6.  My boyfriend is very clumsy. When we go dancing, he keeps on ___stepping to dance___ on my feet. If he doesn't start ___dancing___ more gracefully, I'm going to stop ___going___ dancing with him.

Listen and choose the correct answer.

1. a. delivering babies.
    b. fix broken legs.

2. a. eating junk food.
    b. to pay our bills late.

3. a. swimming.
    b. to play golf.

4. a. to tap dance.
    b. figure skating.

5. a. to work out at a
        health club every
        week.
    b. retiring.

6. a. taking karate lessons.
    b. mend my pants.

7. a. to go back to college?
    b. moving?

8. a. to argue with people.
    b. biting my nails.

9. a. teasing your sister?
    b. to go to bed so late?

10. a. eat fruits and
        vegetables.
    b. worrying about my
        health all the time.

11. a. stand in line.
    b. wearing a suit.

12. a. taking photographs?
    b. study the piano?

13. a. to assemble his VCR.
    b. clean his apartment.

14. a. studying engineering.
    b. teach a computer
        course.

15. a. to live at home.
    b. going to school for the
        rest of your life.

O **WHAT DOES IT MEAN?**

Choose the correct answer.

1. My wife is very dizzy.
    a. I'm glad to hear that.
    b. How long has she been feeling sick?
    c. I guess she has a lot of things to do.

2. Peter and Nancy are vegetarians.
    a. They've quit eating vegetables.
    b. They've stopped planting flowers.
    c. They've stopped eating meat.

3. Andrew avoids talking about politics.
    a. He doesn't like talking about politics.
    b. He enjoys talking about politics.
    c. He's learning to talk about politics.

4. Shirley has worked her way to the top.
    a. She's the tallest person in her family.
    b. She's the president of her company.
    c. She works on the top floor of her building.

5. The people across the street were furious.
    a. They were embarrassed.
    b. They were awkward.
    c. They were very angry.

6. What's your present occupation?
    a. What do you do now?
    b. What are you going to do?
    c. What did you do when you were young?

7. This is my father-in-law, Mr. Kramer.
    a. He just graduated from high school.
    b. He just retired.
    c. He's seventeen years old.

8. My mother is going to mend my socks.
    a. She's going to fix them.
    b. She's going to wash them.
    c. She's going to send them to my sister.

9. You should stop gossiping.
    a. You should stop interrupting people.
    b. You should stop bumping into people.
    c. You should stop talking about people.

10. I've decided to ask for a raise.
    a. You should speak to your landlord.
    b. You should speak to your boss.
    c. You should speak to your instructor.

11. Dr. Wu has a lot of patients.
    a. That's true. She never gets angry.
    b. I know. She's a very popular doctor.
    c. That's true. She never gets sick.

12. My Uncle Gino has an Italian accent.
    a. He bought it when he went to Italy.
    b. He wears it all the time.
    c. Everybody knows he's from Italy.

1. Lisa didn't feel very well when she got up this morning because

   she *(eat)* __had__ __eaten__ a lot of candy before she went to bed.

2. My husband invited his boss for dinner last Friday night, and he forgot to tell me.

   Unfortunately, I *(get)* _____ already _____ tickets for a concert.

3. Our friends didn't stop showing us pictures of their grandson all evening. They

   (visit) _____ just _____ him the day before.

4. I wanted to drive to the mountains with my friends yesterday, but they *(drive)* _____

   _____ to the mountains the afternoon before.

5. Andrew wasn't very happy when I visited him yesterday. He *(cut)* _____ just _____
   himself while he was cooking dinner.

6. Alice couldn't buy the new printer she wanted because she *(spend)* _____ _____
   all her money on her vacation.

7. When my son got home from his date last night, my wife and I *(go)* _____ already

   _____ to sleep.

8. My children didn't want to eat pancakes for breakfast yesterday morning because

   I *(make)* _____ _____ pancakes the morning before.

9. I didn't see a movie with my friends last weekend because I *(see)* _____ _____
   three movies the weekend before.

10. When I got up this morning, my wife *(leave)* _____ already _____ for work.

11. Norman was upset when I saw him yesterday morning. He *(have)* _____ _____
    a big argument with his next-door neighbor the night before.

12. When I saw Jill today, she was very happy. Her boyfriend *(give)* _____ just _____
    her a beautiful bracelet for her birthday.

13. Tom couldn't lend me his dictionary the other day because he *(lose)* _____ _____
    it the week before.

B GRAMMARRAP: *Never Before*

Listen. Then clap and practice.

She felt very   happy   when she left   the store.
She had never   bought   a computer   before.

He looked   very nervous when he knocked   on the door.
He had never   gone out   on a date   before.

She felt very   weak,   and her throat was   sore.
She had never   had   the flu   before.

He felt   very proud   when his guests asked for   more.
He had never   baked   a pie   before.

She felt   very foolish   when her food   hit the floor.
She had never   eaten   with chopsticks   before.

He looked   very scared   when it started to   roar.
He had never   been close   to a lion   before.

She was very   annoyed   when he started to   snore.
He had never   made   so much noise   before.

He was very   surprised   when he opened   the drawer.
He had never   seen   so much money   before.

Gary Gray was very upset yesterday. He didn't get up until 9:00, and as a result, he was late for everything all day!

Today's meeting begins at 10:00.

2. He drove to the office and arrived late for an important meeting.

It _____ already _____.

Bank Closes at 3:00.

4. He got to the bank at 3:15, but he was too late. It _____ already _____.

To: garyg@go.com
From: tom@hopmail.com

I'll be leaving at 4:30. Hope to see you before then.

6. He had made plans to get together with his friend Tom. But he didn't get to Tom's office until 5:00. His friend Tom

_____ already _____.

Last train to Centerville leaves at 9:30.

1. He got to the train station at 9:45. The train __had__ already ____left____.

To: garyg@go.com
From: janet@hopmail.com

Let's have lunch at 12:00. I have to go back to work at 12:45.

3. He got to the restaurant at 1:00 to meet his friend Janet for lunch. However, she

_____ already _____ back to work.

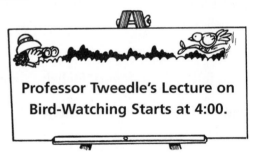

Professor Tweedle's Lecture on Bird-Watching Starts at 4:00.

5. He got to the bird-watching lecture at 4:15. It _____ already _____.

Dear Gary,
    Our plane will be arriving at the airport at 8:10. We're looking forward to seeing you.
        Love,
        Grandma & Grandpa

7. He drove to the airport to pick up his grandmother and grandfather. He got to the airport at 8:30. Their plane

_____ already _____.

1. We got lost on the way to the party last night. We *(listen)* ___hadn't___ ___listened___ very carefully to the directions.

2. I enjoyed seeing my old friends at my high school reunion last weekend.

   I *(see)* _____ _____ them since we finished high school.

3. My wife and I decided to have a picnic in the park last Sunday. We *(have)* _____

   _____ a picnic in the park in a long time.

4. I went dancing with my girlfriend last Saturday night, and I hurt my back.

   I *(go)* _____ _____ dancing in a long time.

5. Cynthia was embarrassed at her party last night. She had invited her cousin Charles, but

   she *(remember)* _____ _____ to invite his girlfriend, Louise.

6. Frank looked terrible when I saw him yesterday. His pants were dirty, he

   (iron) _____ _____ his shirt, and he *(shave)* _____ _____
   in several days.

7. Michael was very discouraged when I saw him last week. He had been on a diet for a month,

   and he *(lose)* _____ _____ any weight.

8. Sylvia fell several times while she was skiing last weekend. She *(ski)* _____

   _____ in a long time.

9. Arnold's boss fired him last week. Arnold *(get)* _____ _____ to work on time
   in six months.

10. Betty was very lucky she didn't miss her plane this morning. She got to the airport late, but

    the plane *(take off)* _____ _____ yet.

11. Alan did poorly on his English exam last week. I'm not surprised. He *(study)* _____

    _____ for the test.

12. Stuart enjoyed riding his bicycle last weekend. He *(ride)* _____ _____ it in a
    long time.

Jennifer was very busy after school yesterday.

1:00	write an English composition
2:00	study for my science test
3:00	practice the trombone
4:00	read the next history chapter
5:00	memorize my lines for the school play

What was she doing at 2:00?

1. _____ She was studying for her science test. _____

What had she already done?

2. _____ She had already written an English composition. _____

What hadn't she done yet?

3. _____ She hadn't practiced the trombone yet. _____

4. _____

5. _____

Brian had a very busy day at the office yesterday.

9:00	send an e-mail to the boss
10:00	give the employees their paychecks
11:00	hook up the new printer
1:00	write to the Bentley Company
2:00	take two packages to the post office

What was he doing at 11:00?

6. _____

What had he already done?

7. _____

8. _____

What hadn't he done yet?

9. _____

10. _____

Mr. and Mrs. Mendoza had a very busy day at home yesterday.

8:00	assemble Billy's new bicycle
9:00	fix the fence
11:00	clean the garage
2:00	repair the roof
4:00	start to build a tree house

What were they doing at 11:00?

11. _____

What had they already done?

12. _____

13. _____

What hadn't they done yet?

14. _____

15. _____

Brenda wants to lose some weight, so she had a very busy day at her health club.

9:00	do yoga
10:00	go jogging
12:00	play squash
3:00	lift weights
4:00	swim across the pool 10 times

What was she doing at 12:00?

16. _____

What had she already done?

17. _____

18. _____

What hadn't she done yet?

19. _____

20. _____

F WHAT HAD THEY BEEN DOING?

1. Professor Smith finally ended his lecture at 6:00. He *(talk)* _____ had been talking _____ for three hours.

2. The Millers moved out of their apartment building last week. They *(live)* _____ _____ there for several years.

3. Our daughter lost her job last week. She *(work)* _____ at the same company since she graduated from college.

4. Peter was happy when he and his girlfriend finally got married. They *(go out)* _____ _____ for eight years.

5. We were sad when Rudy's Restaurant closed. We *(plan)* _____ to eat there on our anniversary.

6. We felt very nostalgic when we went back to our hometown. We *(think about)* _____ _____ going back there for a long time.

7. My husband and I were happy when our son decided to study harder. He *(get)* _____ _____ poor grades in school.

8. Mr. Best was happy when his neighbor bought his own ladder. He *(borrow)* _____ _____ Mr. Best's ladder for many years.

9. I'm not surprised that Lenny's doctor put him on a diet. Lenny *(eat)* _____ too many fatty foods.

10. It's too bad your daughter wasn't able to perform in her violin recital last weekend. She

    (rehearse) _____ for it for a long time.

11. I'm sorry you had to cancel your trip to Hawaii. You and your wife *(look forward)* _____ _____ to it for a long time.

12. I'm so happy that Sally won the marathon last weekend. She *(train)* _____ for it for the past six months.

13. Nobody at the office was surprised when Mrs. Anderson fired Frank, her new assistant. He

    (arrive) _____ late for work every day for the past month.

GRAMMARRAP: *George Had Been Thinking of Studying Greek*

Listen. Then clap and practice.

George had been thinking of studying Greek,
Moving to Athens and learning to speak.
But he changed his mind and decided to stay
With his family and friends and his dog in L.A.

Jill had been planning to learn how to ski,
But she tripped and fell and sprained her knee.
She had been dreaming of mountains and snow.
But now she's at home and has no place to go.

Marie had been planning to marry Tim,
But she fell in love with his brother, Jim.
Jim had been thinking of marrying Dee,
But everything changed when he met Marie.

H **LISTENING**

Listen to each word and then say it.

1. re<u>ti</u>re
2. memo<u>r</u>ize
3. p<u>r</u>actice
4. <u>d</u>rug sto<u>r</u>e
5. favo<u>r</u>ite
6. inter<u>r</u>upt
7. a<u>r</u>ound
8. <u>r</u>estau<u>r</u>ant

9. live<u>l</u>y
10. <u>l</u>oud<u>l</u>y
11. swo<u>ll</u>en
12. e<u>l</u>evator
13. f<u>l</u>y
14. be<u>l</u>ieve
15. co<u>l</u>d
16. fa<u>ll</u> as<u>l</u>eep

1 MARYLOU'S BROKEN KEYBOARD

Marylou's keyboard is broken. The r's and the l's don't always work. Fill in the missing r's and l's, and then read Marylou's letters aloud.

1.

_R_oger,

I'm af_r_aid the__e's something w__ong with the fi__ep__ace in the __iving __oom. A__so, the __ef__ige__ato__ is b__oken. I've been ca____ing the __and__o__d fo__ th__ee days on his ce____ phone, but he hasn't ca____ed back. I hope he ca____s me tomo____ow.

Ma__y__ou

2.

__ouise,

I'm te____ib__y wo____ied about my b__othe__ La____y's hea__th. He hu__t his __eg whi__e he was p__aying baseba____. He had a____eady dis__ocated his shou__der whi__e he was su__fing __ast F__iday. Acco__ding to his docto__, he is a__so having p__ob__ems with his b__ood p__essu__e and with his __ight w__ist. He __ea____y should t__y to __e__ax and take __ife a __itt__e easie__.

Ma__y__ou

3.

A__no__d,

Can you possib__y __ecommend a good __estau__ant in you__ neighbo__hood? I'm p__anning on taking my re__atives to __unch tomo____ow, but I'm not su__e whe__e.

We ate at a ve__y nice G__eek __estau__ant nea__ you__ apa__tment bui__ding __ast month, but I haven't been ab__e to __emembe__ the name. Do you know the p__ace?

You__ f__iend,

Ma__y__ou

4.

__osa,

I have been p__anning a t__ip to F__o__ida. I'____ be f__ying to O____ando on F__iday, and I'____ be __etu__ning th__ee days __ater. Have you eve__ been the__e? I __emembe__ you had fami__y membe__s who __ived in F__o__ida seve__a__ yea__s ago.

P__ease w__ite back.

A____ my __ove,

Ma__y__ou

Listen and choose the correct answer.

1. a. He can't find it anywhere.
    b. Where can it be?
    c. Nobody can hear him.

2. a. No, she isn't. She's my wife.
    b. Yes. She's my wife's cousin.
    c. No. She works for a different company.

3. a. Did you take a lot of photographs?
    b. Why did you charge it?
    c. That's too bad. You had been looking forward to it.

4. a. I know. He missed all his tests.
    b. I know. He's been doing very poorly.
    c. I know. He hasn't had a bad grade yet.

5. a. Did she find it?
    b. Whose is it?
    c. I'm sure it hurt a lot.

6. a. We stayed for the lecture.
    b. We talked about classical music.
    c. We read about psychology.

7. a. Did you enjoy yourselves?
    b. How many miles did you travel?
    c. Where did you drive?

8. a. She's having problems with her feet.
    b. She's having problems with her teeth.
    c. That's okay. We all make mistakes.

9. a. Did he make it?
    b. When did you get home?
    c. I know. He likes everything you serve.

10. a. You're right. I bought one.
    b. No, but I heard the noise.
    c. Sorry. We don't sell motorcycles.

11. a. I think so. He's been working hard.
    b. Yes. His plane will leave soon.
    c. I hope so. He never goes to work.

12. a. Poor Amy! She's always sick.
    b. Amy needs a new pair of boots.
    c. She was afraid to ask for it.

13. a. What a shame! Now she can't sing.
    b. What a shame! Now she can't knit.
    c. What a shame! Now she can't walk.

14. a. Would you like to talk about it?
    b. Who are you going to give it to?
    c. What did you decide to do?

15. a. I like you, too.
    b. What are you going to send me?
    c. You don't have anything to be jealous about.

16. a. Was it a very bad accident?
    b. Do you know anybody who can fix it?
    c. How long had they been going out?

17. a. I hope he feels better soon.
    b. What happened? Did you twist it?
    c. How are your cousins?

18. a. Did you call the doctor?
    b. What had you eaten?
    c. Why were you sad?

19. a. I'm glad to hear that.
    b. What was he angry about?
    c. What did he ask them?

20. a. We enjoyed the music.
    b. The lecture was very boring.
    c. The food was excellent.

21. a. They're too small.
    b. You have a job interview today.
    c. You have a baseball game today.

22. a. She enjoys going to the symphony.
    b. She enjoys going window-shopping.
    c. She enjoys doing gymnastics.

23. a. We're going to have a party.
    b. We're going on vacation.
    c. We received a lot of anniversary gifts.

24. a. He's glad he bought it.
    b. He's going to wear it for several years.
    c. He has to return it on Tuesday.

✓ CHECK-UP TEST: Chapters 7–8

A. Complete the sentences with the appropriate verb form.

(eat) 1. Why do you keep on _____ing_____ junk food?

(wrestle) 2. My mother thinks _____ing_____ is dangerous.

(stop) 3. I've decided _____to_____ interrupting people all the time.

(box) 4. Bruno practices _____ing_____ every day at the gym.

(swim) 5. _____ is a good way to relax.

(skate) 6. Where did your daughter learn _____to_____ so well?

(talk) 7. Please stop _____ing_____. I'm trying to sleep!

(do) 8. Rita thinks that _____doing_____ exercises is a good way to start the day.

B. Complete the sentences, using the past perfect tense.

Ex. (wear) I wore my favorite striped tie to work yesterday. I __hadn't worn__ it to work in a long time.

(start) By the time Andrew got to the play, it __had__ already __started__.

(speak) 1. I had dinner with some Japanese friends last night. I enjoyed myself very much

because I __hadn't spoken__ Japanese in a long time.

(do) 2. By the time Jennifer's father got home from work, she __had__ already

__had__ her homework, and she was ready to play baseball in the yard with him.

(leave) 3. Ronald was upset. By the time he got to the train, it __had__ already

__left__.

(write) 4. I wrote an e-mail to my grandparents last night because I __hadn't written__ to them for a few weeks.

(have) 5. Patty had pizza for lunch yesterday. She __hadn't had__ pizza in a long time.

(take) 6. My husband and I took a walk after dinner last night. We __hadn't taken__ a walk after dinner in a long time.

(eat) 7. I ate a big piece of chocolate cake last night and felt terrible about it. I __hadn't__

__eaten__ a rich dessert since I started my diet.

(go) 8. My parents went back to their hometown last month. They __hadn't gone__ back there for twenty years.

C. Complete the sentences, using the past perfect continuous tense.

Ex. *(study)*   Jonathan was glad he did well on his astronomy exam. He _____had been studying_____ for it for days.

(work)   **1.**   Marvin didn't get his promotion at work. He was heartbroken because he

_____ overtime for several months.

(train)   **2.**   I was disappointed they canceled the marathon last week. I _____

_____ for it since last summer.

(argue)   **3.**   Jane and John broke up last night. They _____
with each other for the past several weeks.

(plan)   **4.**   Nancy caught a cold and couldn't go on her camping trip. It's a shame because she

_____ it since last April.

D. Listen and choose the correct answer.

Ex.   (a.)   go fishing.
     b.   going canoeing.

1.   a.   tease her little brother.
     (b.)   interrupting people.

2.   (a.)   moving to Miami.
     b.   to sell our house.

3.   a.   to buy a sports car.
     (b.)   buying a sports car.

4.   a.   waiting in line.
     (b.)   drive downtown.

5.   (a.)   going out with Richard.
     b.   ask for a raise.

WHAT ARE THEY SAYING?

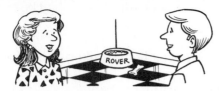

1. A. Did you pick up Rover at the vet?

   B. No. I didn't _____pick him up_____.
   I thought YOU did.

2. A. Did you turn on the heat?

   B. Yes. I __turned it on__ a few
   hours ago, but it's still cold in here.

3. A. You should take back these library
   books.

   B. I know. I'll __take them back__
   tomorrow morning.

4. A. Has Diane filled out her income tax
   forms?

   B. No. She's going to __fill it out__
   this weekend.

5. A. Where should we hang up this
   portrait?

   B. Let's __hang it up__
   over the fireplace.

6. A. I'm having trouble hooking up my
   computer.

   B. No problem. I'll __hook it up__.

7. A. Are you ever going to throw out these
   old souvenirs?

   B. I'll __throw them out__
   some day.

8. A. Did Sally take back her cell phone to
   the store?

   B. Yes. She __took it back__
   this afternoon.

9. A. Did your daughter take down the
   photographs of her old boyfriend?

   B. Yes. She __took them down__
   as soon as they stopped going out.

10. A. Did you remember to call up Aunt
    Clara to wish her "Happy Birthday"?

    B. Sorry. I didn't __call her up__.
    I forgot it was her birthday.

| bring back | hand in | put away | put on | take off | turn off | turn on | wake up |

1. I think we should __turn on__ the air conditioner. It's getting very hot in here.

Good idea. I'll __turn it on__ right away.

2. When are you going to __hand__ your biology report __in__?

I'm going to __hand it in__ tomorrow morning. I have to write it tonight.

3. Let's __call up__ Mom and Dad! It's 8:00, and they're still sleeping!

Don't __call them up__. It's Saturday. They don't go to work today.

4. Don't forget to __turn__ the printer __off__ before you leave the office tonight.

You don't have to worry. I always __turn it off__ before I leave.

5. Why don't you __take off__ your hat and coat? It's warm in here.

I'll __take them off__ in a few minutes. I'm still a little cold.

6. Susie, when are you going to __put__ your toys __away__?

I'm still playing with them. I'll __put them away__ later.

7. Teddy, it's time for bed. __put__ your pajamas __on__!

Okay, Dad. I'll _____ in a few minutes.

8. Do you think Richard will __bring__ his girlfriend __back__ to the house after the dance?

I don't know. Maybe he'll __bring her back__. I hope he does. I really want to meet her.

C GRAMMARRAP: *I Don't Know How!*

Listen. Then clap and practice.

A. Take off your skis.
Take them off now!

B. I can't take them off.
I don't know how!

A. Turn off the engine!
Turn it off now!

B. I can't turn it off.
I don't know how!

A. Turn on the oven!
Turn it on now!

B. I can't turn it on.
I don't know how!

A. Hook up the printer!
Hook it up now!

B. I can't hook it up.
I don't know how!

A. Pick up the suitcase.
Give it to Jack.

B. I can't pick it up.
I have a bad back!

A. Take back the videos!
Take them back today.

B. I can't take them back.
It's a holiday!

D WHAT ARE THEY SAYING?

cross out	give back	look up	throw away	turn off
do over	hook up	think over	turn down	write down

1.

   Did your teacher like the composition you wrote about Australian birds?

   No, she didn't. I have to _____do it over_____.

2. A. Do we still have the hammer we borrowed from our next-door neighbors?

   B. No, we don't. We ___gave them back___ a long time ago.

3. A. What's the matter with the answering machine? Is it broken?

   B. No, it isn't. I forgot to ___hook it up___.

4. A. Are you going to accept the invitation to Roger's wedding?

   B. I don't know. I have to ___think it over___ carefully. His wedding is in Alaska.

5. A. What's the weather forecast for tomorrow?

   B. I'm not sure. You should ___look it up___ on the Internet.

6. A. Is Kimberly going to the prom with Frank?

   B. No, she isn't. She had to ___turn him down___ because she already had a date with somebody else.

7. A. What should I do with all these letters from my ex-boyfriend?

   B. I think you should ___throw them away___.

8. A. What's Walter's new address?

   B. I can't remember. But I know I've ___write it down___ somewhere.

9. A. Should I erase all these mistakes in my math homework?

   B. No, I think you should just ___cross them out___.

10. Why aren't you watching the president's speech on TV?

    I watched it for a while, but it was boring. So I ___turn it off___.

E WHAT'S THE WORD?

James just moved into a new apartment. What does he have to do?

1. He has to (put away) / throw away his books and his clothes.

2. He has to fill out / (hook up) his printer and his computer.

3. He has to take out / (take back) the moving truck he rented.

Jennifer is very happy and excited. She just got engaged. What's she going to do?

4. She's going to (wake up) / drop off her parents and tell them the news.

5. She's going to call off / (call up) all her friends.

6. She's going to look up / (write down) all the things her boyfriend said.

Mr. and Mrs. Baker's aunt and uncle are going to visit them next week. What do the Bakers have to do before then?

7. They have to clean up / take out their apartment.

8. They have to pick out / put away their children's toys.

9. They have to (throw out) / hook up all their old newspapers.

10. They have to call up / hang up their aunt and uncle's portrait.

F WHAT SHOULD THEY DO?

figure out	look up	throw out	use up
give back	think over	turn off	wake up

1. Abigail, will you marry me?

   That's a big decision, Howard. I have to _____think it over_____.

2. A. I've been using my neighbor's screwdriver all summer.

   B. Don't you think it's time to _____give it back_____?

3. A. Is there any more sugar?

   B. No. We _____used it up_____. We have to buy some tomorrow.

4. A. I don't know the definition of this word.

   B. You really should _____look it up_____ in the dictionary.

5. A. This math problem is very difficult.

   B. Maybe your mother can help you _____figure it out_____.

6. A. It's 7:30, and the children are still sleeping.

   B. They're going to be late for school. I'll _____wake them up_____.

7. A. It's really cold in here! Is the air conditioner on?

   B. Yes, it is. I'll _____ right away.

8. A. I'm very embarrassed. These are the worst photographs anyone has ever taken of me.

   B. Well, if they bother you that much, why don't you _____throw them out_____?

G LISTENING

Listen and choose the correct answer.

1. a. picked it up.
   b. used it up. .

2. a. turn it down.
   b. turn it on.

3. a. take them down.
   b. turn them down.

4. a. think them over.
   b. drop them off.

5. a. hook it up.
   b. look it up.

6. a. give it back?
   b. hand it in?

7. a. throw it out.
   b. figure it out.

8. a. write it down.
   b. use it up.

9. a. pick it up.
   b. clean it up.

H COME UP WITH THE RIGHT ANSWER

call on	get over	look through	pick on	take after
get along with	hear from	look up to	run into	

1. I ____take after____ my father. We're both athletic, we're both interested in engineering, and we both like to paint. I'm really

glad I ____take after him____.

2. I haven't ____heard from____ my son in three weeks. He's

at college, and I usually _____ every week!

3. I'm so embarrassed. My teacher ____called on____ me twice in class today, but I didn't know ANY of the answers. I have to study

tonight. She might _____ again tomorrow.

4. My husband and I enjoyed ____look through____ our wedding

pictures. We hadn't _____ in years.

5. Jack ____got over____ his cold very quickly. I think he

____got over it____ fast because he stayed home and took care of himself.

6. I really ____look up to____ my grandmother. She's honest, she's intelligent, and she's very generous. I hope someday when I'm a

grandmother, my grandchildren will ____look up to____, too.

7. I was very surprised. I ____ran into____ my old girlfriend at the

bank yesterday morning. And then I ____ran into her____ again at a movie last night.

8. I don't ____get along with____ my mother-in-law. We often

disagree. All the people in our family _____.
Why can't I?

9. Bobby is mean. He ____picks on____ his cats all the time.

The cats don't like it when Bobby _____.

I GRAMMARRAP: *I Don't Get Along with Kate and Clem*

Listen. Then clap and practice.

I don't   get along with   Kate and   Clem.
I almost   never   hear from   them.
But I get along   well   with Bob   and Fay.
I call them   up   three times   a day.

Jack   takes after   his Uncle   Jim.
Bob   looks up to   his father,   Tim.
Kate never   picks on   her sister,   Sue.
But she always   picks on   her brother,   Lou.

J CHOOSE

1. A. Do we have any more pens?
    B. No, we don't. We _____.
        a. ran into them
        b. ran out of them ⟲

2. A. Does Carol still have the flu?
    B. No. She _____ a few days ago.
        a. got over it ⟲
        b. got it over

3. A. Does Jill get along with her brother?
    B. No. He _____ all the time.
        a. picks her on
        b. picks on her ⟲

4. A. I can't remember Tom's phone number.
    B. You should _____.
        a. look up to him
        b. look it up ⟲

5. A. Amy knows all the answers in class.
    B. Does the teacher always _____?
        a. call on her ⟲
        b. call her on

6. A. This is a very difficult problem.
    B. I know. I can't _____.
        a. figure out it
        b. figure it out ⟲

7. A. Have you heard from Pam recently?
    B. Yes. I _____ the other day.
        a. heard her from
        b. heard from her ⟲

8. A. What should I do with these old letters?
    B. Why don't you _____?
        a. throw them out ⟲
        b. throw out them

9. A. These photographs are wonderful!
    B. I know. Let's _____ again.
        a. look through them ⟲
        b. look them through

10. A. Do you like William?
    B. Oh, yes. I _____ very well.
        a. get him along
        b. get along with him ⟲

11. A. Should I turn off the computer?
    B. No. You can _____.
        a. leave it on ⟲
        b. leave on it

12. A. Did you hang up your uncle's portrait?
    B. No, I didn't. I _____.
        a. took it down ⟲
        b. took down it

13. A. You look like your father.
    B. I know. Everybody says I _____.
        a. take him after
        b. take after him ⟲

14. A. They have a very unusual last name.
    B. You'll remember it if you _____.
        a. write down it
        b. write it down ⟲

WHAT DOES IT MEAN?

Choose the correct answer.

1. Richard takes after his mother.
   a. He's always with her.
   b. They're both shy.
   c. His mother always arrives first.

2. Please turn off the air conditioner.
   a. It's too hot in this room.
   b. The room is too small.
   c. It's too cold in this room.

3. Tom left his briefcase on the plane.
   a. Maybe his mind slipped.
   b. He forgot it.
   c. He was very careful.

4. I'm going to take these pants back.
   a. They're new.
   b. They're medium.
   c. They're too baggy.

5. Fran can't find her notebook.
   a. I hope she didn't throw it out.
   b. I hope she didn't fill it out.
   c. I hope she didn't take it off.

6. Bob doesn't get along with his neighbors.
   a. He can't stand to talk to them.
   b. He likes them very much.
   c. He looks up to them.

7. I hope I don't run into my old boyfriend.
   a. Why? Will he get hurt?
   b. Why don't you want to see him?
   c. Why? Does he like to jog?

8. Paul had to do his homework over.
   a. It was excellent.
   b. He didn't think it over.
   c. He had made a lot of mistakes.

L **LISTENING**

Listen and choose the correct answer.

1. a. He's very tall.
   b. I can never find him.
   c. I want to be like him.

2. a. You're lucky he has a car.
   b. I'm sure that bothers you.
   c. Do you also pick him up?

3. a. Yes. I put it in the closet.
   b. Yes. I gave it to our neighbor.
   c. Yes. We had used it all up.

4. a. I'm sorry you're still sick.
   b. I'm glad you're feeling better.
   c. It's too bad you have to do it over.

5. a. No. He speaks very softly.
   b. Yes. He sent me an e-mail yesterday.
   c. No. I haven't heard him recently.

6. a. The music was very loud.
   b. Somebody had picked it up.
   c. I already had another date.

7. a. Yes, several times.
   b. Yes, but I wasn't home.
   c. Yes, but I had already left the house.

8. a. He didn't need it anymore.
   b. It was already at the cleaner's.
   c. I know. He found one he really liked.

9. a. Did she hurt herself?
   b. How did you hurt yourself?
   c. When does her plane leave?

10. a. The store isn't having a sale.
    b. Everything in the store is cheaper.
    c. Everything is 20 cents less this week.

11. a. Good. I'll buy it.
    b. Don't worry. We have larger ones.
    c. I know. It's too tight.

12. a. Yes. I used up four pair.
    b. Yes. I put on four pair.
    c. Yes. I looked up four pair.

1.
   I ate too much. So ___did I___.

2.
   I hate to go to the mall. _____, too.

3.
   I can play the trombone. So _____.

4.
   I'm allergic to milk. _____, too.

5.
   I'll be starting college this fall. _____, too.

6.
   I was late for work. So _____.

7.
   I'm going to retire soon. So _____.

8.
   I've been doing poorly in school recently. _____, too.

9.
   I just got a promotion. _____, too.

10.
    I'll be on vacation next week. So _____.

11. I have to lose a little weight. So _____.

A. Do you live near here?

B. Yes. I live on Center Street.

A. Really? So ___do I___ [1]. I live in the new apartment building at the corner of Center Street and Broadway.

B. What a coincidence! _____ [2], too. I guess we're neighbors. My name is Frank Winters.

A. Hi. I'm Steve Green. Nice to meet you.

B. Nice meeting you, too. So how long have you been living there?

A. I moved in last week.

B. What a coincidence! _____ [3], too. I've been very busy since I got here.

A. So _____ [4]. Moving into a new apartment isn't easy.

B. You're right. It isn't. Tell me, have you found a job yet?

A. Yes, I have. I'll be working at Mason's Department Store.

B. I don't believe it! _____ [5], too.

A. What department will you be working in?

B. I got a job in the Men's Clothing Department.

A. What a coincidence! So _____ [6]. I was a salesperson in my last job also.

B. _____ [7], too. I sold men's clothing.

A. I can't believe it! _____ [8], too.

B. I'm on my way to work right now.

A. _____ [9], too. Do you want to have lunch together?

B. Sure. I have a lunch break at noon.

A. So _____ [10]. Let's meet for lunch in the company cafeteria.

B. Okay. That'll be nice. I'm looking forward to it.

A. So _____ [11].

1. I didn't like the movie.
   Neither _____did I_____.

2. I'm not feeling very well.
   _____ either.

3. I wasn't in school yesterday.
   Neither _____.

4. I can't play tennis very well.
   _____ either.

5. I won't be home tonight.
   _____ either.

6. I've never been in the hospital before.
   Neither _____.

7. I can't stand driving in traffic.
   _____ either.

8. I'm not going to order dessert.
   Neither _____.

9. I didn't enjoy the lecture.
   _____ either.

10. I don't like to practice the piano.
    Neither _____.

11. I'll never go sailing again.
    Neither _____.

Listen and complete the sentences.

1. So ____did I____ .

2. _____ , too.

3. So _____ .

4. _____ either.

5. _____ , too.

6. _____ , too.

7. Neither _____ .

8. _____ , too.

9. Neither _____ .

10. So _____ .

11. _____ either.

12. _____ , too.

13. Neither _____ .

14. So _____ .

15. _____ either.

E **GRAMMARRAP:** *So Do I*

Listen. Then clap and practice.

A. I like to   fly.

B. So do   I.

A. They like to   ski.

B. So do   we.

A. She likes the   zoo.

B. He does,   too.

A. You're a good   friend.

B. So are   you.

F **GRAMMARRAP:** *They Didn't Either*

Listen. Then clap and practice.

We didn't   eat it.

They didn't   either.

He didn't   finish it.

Neither did   she.

She wasn't   hungry.

He wasn't   either.

They weren't   hungry.

Neither were   we.

G WHAT ARE THEY SAYING?

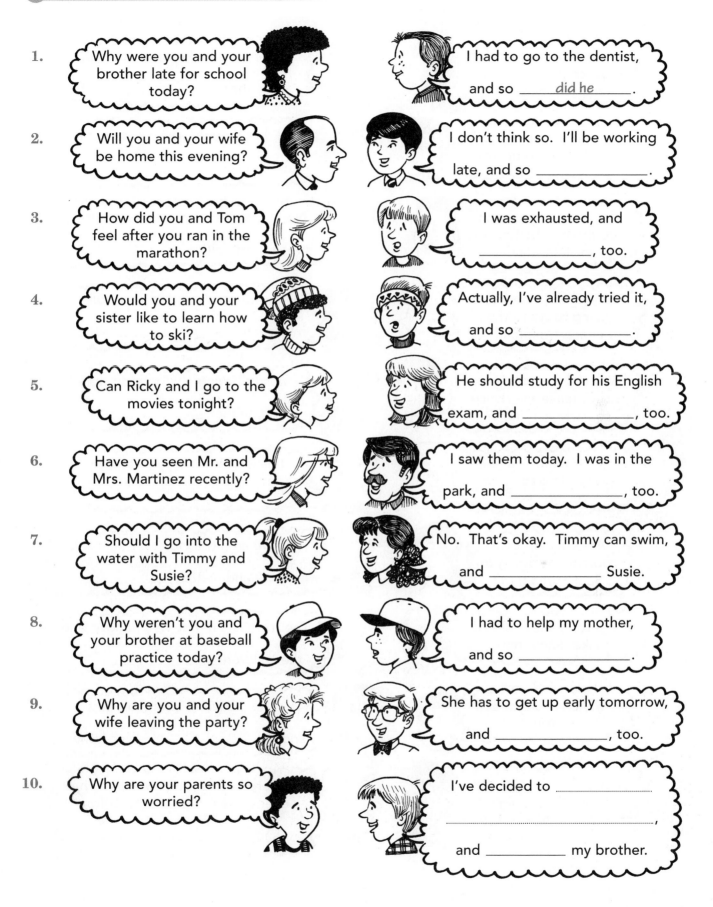

1. Why were you and your brother late for school today?

   I had to go to the dentist, and so ____did he____.

2. Will you and your wife be home this evening?

   I don't think so. I'll be working late, and so _____.

3. How did you and Tom feel after you ran in the marathon?

   I was exhausted, and _____, too.

4. Would you and your sister like to learn how to ski?

   Actually, I've already tried it, and so _____.

5. Can Ricky and I go to the movies tonight?

   He should study for his English exam, and _____, too.

6. Have you seen Mr. and Mrs. Martinez recently?

   I saw them today. I was in the park, and _____, too.

7. Should I go into the water with Timmy and Susie?

   No. That's okay. Timmy can swim, and _____ Susie.

8. Why weren't you and your brother at baseball practice today?

   I had to help my mother, and so _____.

9. Why are you and your wife leaving the party?

   She has to get up early tomorrow, and _____, too.

10. Why are your parents so worried?

    I've decided to ...., and _____ my brother.

Activity Workbook 113

1. Are you and your brother going to be in the school play?

   Unfortunately, he can't act, and neither ____can I____.

2. Why do you and your friends look so upset?

   I didn't do very well on the math test, and _____ either.

3. Did you and your son see the baseball game on TV today?

   No, we didn't. I'm not interested in sports, and neither _____.

4. Are you and your sister going to go to the concert tonight?

   No, we aren't. I don't like folk music, and _____ either.

5. Why did you and your friends leave the dance so early last night?

   I wasn't having a very good time, and neither _____.

6. Have you and your wife made plans for your vacation yet?

   I haven't had very much time, and _____ either.

7. Are you and your roommates going to Sally's wedding?

   No, we aren't. I won't be here this weekend, and neither _____.

8. It's getting late. Should I make dinner now?

   The truth is, I'm not very hungry, and the children _____.

9. Is the DVD player still broken?

   Yes, it is. I haven't been able to fix it, and _____ your father.

10. How was your date with Samantha last night?

    We were both a little nervous. I had never gone out on a date before, and _____ either.

WHAT ARE THEY SAYING?

so	too	either	neither

1. A. Why didn't Ronald and his wife go to work yesterday?

   B. He had a terrible cold,

   and {
   so did she .
   she did, too .
   }

2. A. Did Betty and Bob enjoy the concert last night?

   B. Not really. She couldn't hear the music,

   and {
   neither could he .
   he couldn't either .
   }

3. A. Do Jack and his girlfriend enjoy going sailing?

   B. No, they don't. She gets seasick,

   and {
   he does too .
   so does he .
   }

4. A. Why didn't Mr. and Mrs. Miller order the cheesecake for dessert?

   B. He doesn't eat rich foods,

   and {
   and she doesn't .
   neither does she .
   }

5. A. Why did Beverly and Brian have trouble doing their chemistry experiments?

   B. He hadn't followed the instructions,

   and {
   neither had she .
   she hadn't either .
   }

6. A. Why aren't you and Peter good friends any more?

   B. I'm in love with Amanda Richardson,

   and {
   he is too .
   _so is he_ .
   }

1. I'm tall, but my sister and brother ___aren't___. I've always ___been___ the tallest person in our family.

2. My brother isn't very athletic, but my sister ___is___. She enjoys ___playing___ squash and ___doing___ gymnastics.

3. I can't draw pictures, but my brother ___can___. He's been ___drawing___ pictures since he ___was___ four years old.

4. My brother and I have different interests. I enjoy seeing movies, but my brother ___doesn't___. He enjoys ___going___ to lectures and concerts.

5. My mother is interested in photography, but my father ___isn't___. My mother ___has been taking___ photographs since she was a teenager.

6. My father has lived here all his life, but his parents ___haven't___. They've ___lived___ in this country ___for___ fifty years. Before that, they ___lived___ in Italy.

7. My grandparents sometimes speak to us in Italian, but my father ___doesn't___. He ___hasn't spoken___ Italian to anyone in a long time.

8. I'll be going to college next year, but my brother ___won't___. He ___hasn't___ finished high school yet.

9. I don't have a very good voice, but my sister ___does___. She sings in the school choir. She has ___sung___ in the choir ___since___ she started high school.

10. I'm usually very neat, but my sister and brother ___aren't___. They never hang ___up___ their clothes or put ___away___ their books.

11. I know how to ski, but my brother ___doesn't___. I've been skiing ___for___ the past nine years.

12. My sister is a very good skater, but my brother and I ___aren't___. We just started ___skating___ a month ago. Before that, we ___had___ never ___skated___ at all.

Listen and complete the sentences.

1. but my husband _____ didn't _____.

2. but my daughter _____ isn't _____.

3. but you _____ won't _____.

4. but I _____ have _____.

5. but my friends _____ can't _____.

6. but my wife _____ doesn't _____.

7. but you _____ haven't _____.

8. but my brother _____ didn't _____.

9. but everybody else _____ will _____

10. but our teacher _____ wasn't _____.

11. but my son _____ is _____.

12. but the other man _____ didn't _____.

13. but my sister _____ can _____.

14. but I _____ don't _____.

15. but my friends _____ will _____.

16. but my brother _____ is _____.

17. but my children _____ have _____.

18. but I _____ was _____.

L **GRAMMARRAP:** *I've Been Working Hard, and You Have, Too*

Listen. Then clap and practice.

I've been working hard, and	you have,	too.
I'm exhausted,	and so	are you.
He's been out of town,	and so	has she.
They've been very busy,	and so	have we.
I didn't go,	and neither	did he.
They weren't there,	and neither	were we.
We stayed home,	and so	did they.
Nobody went	to the meeting	that day.
I don't speak Greek,	but my brother	does.
I wasn't born in Greece,	but my mother	was.
I didn't study Greek,	but my brother	did.
He's spoken Greek	since he was	a kid.

M SOUND IT OUT!

Listen to each word and then say it.

f<u>u</u>ll		f<u>oo</u>l

1. l<u>oo</u>k	3. p<u>u</u>t	1. n<u>oo</u>n	3. J<u>u</u>dy
2. c<u>ou</u>ld	4. f<u>oo</u>t	2. dr<u>ew</u>	4. f<u>oo</u>d

Listen and put a circle around the word that has the same sound.

1. f<u>u</u>ll: p<u>oo</u>l   (cooks)   sh<u>oe</u>
2. fl<u>u</u>:   (t<u>oo</u>)   w<u>ou</u>ld   bl<u>oo</u>d
3. g<u>oo</u>d: s<u>ou</u>p   (sh<u>ou</u>ldn't)   J<u>u</u>ne
4. w<u>oo</u>d: fl<u>u</u>   t<u>oo</u>th   (p<u>u</u>t)
5. c<u>ou</u>ld: c<u>u</u>p   (c<u>oo</u>kies)   upstairs
6. h<u>oo</u>k: f<u>oo</u>d   m<u>o</u>vie   (g<u>oo</u>d)
7. w<u>o</u>man: (s<u>u</u>gar)   tr<u>ue</u>   n<u>ew</u>

Now make a sentence using all the words you circled, and read the sentence aloud.

8. .... much ....
in their ....

9. s<u>ui</u>t: (tw<u>o</u>)   put   bus
10. c<u>oo</u>k: f<u>oo</u>d   (b<u>oo</u>ks)   s<u>u</u>nny
11. f<u>oo</u>t: (b<u>oo</u>kcase)   p<u>oo</u>l   m<u>u</u>st
12. bl<u>ue</u>:   just   (wh<u>o</u>)   l<u>oo</u>ked
13. w<u>ou</u>ld: s<u>ui</u>t   t<u>oo</u>l   (t<u>oo</u>k)
14. c<u>oo</u>l: st<u>oo</u>d   (aftern<u>oo</u>n)   p<u>u</u>lse
15. sch<u>oo</u>l: (S<u>u</u>san's)   th<u>u</u>nder   fl<u>oo</u>r

Now make a sentence using all the words you circled, and read the sentence aloud.

16. .... from ....
.... this .... ?

WHAT DOES IT MEAN?

_j_	1. afford	a. afraid
_c_	2. argue	b. do poorly
_q_	3. bachelor	c. fight
_s_	4. begin	d. finish
_n_	5. bump into	e. friendly and talkative
_h_	6. can't stand	f. give back
_i_	7. compatible	g. give lessons
_x_	8. consider	h. hate
_m_	9. continue	i. have a lot in common
_v_	10. discuss	j. have enough money
_w_	11. exam	k. how much it costs
_y_	12. exhausted	l. hurt
_b_	13. fail	m. keep on
_a_	14. frightened	n. meet
_v_	15. hike	o. ready
_l_	16. injure	p. recently
_p_	17. lately	q. single man
_e_	18. outgoing	r. someone who doesn't eat meat
_o_	19. prepared	s. start
_k_	20. price	t. study again
_f_	21. return	u. take a long walk
_t_	22. review	v. talk about
_z_	23. stand in line	w. test
_g_	24. teach	x. think about
_d_	25. use up	y. tired
_r_	26. vegetarian	z. wait

✓ CHECK-UP TEST: Chapters 9-10

A. Complete the sentences.

Ex. My son is waiting for me at the bus stop. I have to pick ___him___ ___up___ right away.

My mother and I are both tall with curly hair. Everybody says I take ___after___ ___her___.

1. I'll finish my homework in a little while, and then I'll hand ___it___ ___in___.

2. My father is a very smart man. I really look ___up___ ___to___ ___him___.

3. I haven't talked to Aunt Shirley lately. I hope I hear ___how___ ___her___ soon.

4. My English teacher didn't like my composition. I have to do ___it___ ___over___.

5. I don't know the definition of this word. I need to look ___it___ ___up___.

6. I can't find any flour. I think we ran ___out___ ___of___ ___it___.

7. I can't find my wallet. Could you help me look ___for___ ___it___?

8. Don't leave your clothes on the bed. You really should hang ___them___ ___up___.

9. Don't worry about your mistakes. You can always cross ___them___ ___up___.

10. I can never remember Alan's address. I should write ___it___ ___down___.

11. I've had the flu for the past several days. My doctor says I'll get ___over___ ___it___ soon.

B. Complete the sentences.

so	too	neither	either

Ex. Maria did well on her science test, and _____so did_____ her sister.

1. I'm wearing new shoes today, and ___so is___ my brother.

2. I won't be able to come to the meeting tomorrow, and ___neither will___ Barbara.

3. I was bored during Professor Gray's lecture, and my friends ___were, too___.

4. Janet can't skate, and her brother ___can't either___.

5. I've been taking guitar lessons for years, and ___so have___ my sisters.

6. David worked overtime yesterday, and his wife ___did too___.

7. Louise has never been to Europe, and ___neither has___ her husband.

8. I want to complain to the landlord, and ___so do___ my neighbors.

9. I'm not very athletic, and ___neither is___ my wife.

● **120** **Activity Workbook**

C. Listen and complete the sentences.

Ex. but her husband _____ *doesn't* _____.

1. but my sister _____ isn't _____.

2. but my parents _____ will _____.

3. but my brother _____ doesn't _____.

4. but my wife _____ has _____.

5. but I _____ didn't _____.

ACHIEVEMENT TESTS

A PERSONAL INFORMATION FORM

Name: (1) _____

Address: (2) _____

City: (3) _____ State: (4) ____ Zip Code: (5) _____

Social Security Number: (6) _____ Country of Origin: (7) _____

Telephone: (8) _____ E-mail: (9) _____ Date of Birth: (10) _____

Height: (11) ____ Eye Color: (12) ____ Hair Color: (13) ____ Marital Status: (14) ____

Family Members in Household (Name—Relationship):

(15) _____ _____

Look at the information. Choose the correct line on the form.

1. 11/14/88
   - Ⓐ Line 5
   - Ⓑ Line 6
   - Ⓒ Line 8
   - Ⓓ Line 10

2. 224-67-8139
   - Ⓐ Line 5
   - Ⓑ Line 6
   - Ⓒ Line 8
   - Ⓓ Line 10

3. Mexico
   - Ⓐ Line 3
   - Ⓑ Line 4
   - Ⓒ Line 7
   - Ⓓ Line 10

4. 1263 Main St.
   - Ⓐ Line 2
   - Ⓑ Line 7
   - Ⓒ Line 9
   - Ⓓ Line 15

5. 5'9"
   - Ⓐ Line 5
   - Ⓑ Line 6
   - Ⓒ Line 10
   - Ⓓ Line 11

6. married
   - Ⓐ Line 7
   - Ⓑ Line 12
   - Ⓒ Line 14
   - Ⓓ Line 15

7. FL
   - Ⓐ Line 3
   - Ⓑ Line 4
   - Ⓒ Line 5
   - Ⓓ Line 14

8. blue
   - Ⓐ Line 11
   - Ⓑ Line 12
   - Ⓒ Line 13
   - Ⓓ Line 14

9. (305) 965-4213
   - Ⓐ Line 5
   - Ⓑ Line 6
   - Ⓒ Line 8
   - Ⓓ Line 9

10. Alma Suarez—wife
    - Ⓐ Line 1
    - Ⓑ Line 2
    - Ⓒ Line 14
    - Ⓓ Line 15

11. Miami
    - Ⓐ Line 3
    - Ⓑ Line 4
    - Ⓒ Line 5
    - Ⓓ Line 9

12. cjs24@msl.com
    - Ⓐ Line 2
    - Ⓑ Line 3
    - Ⓒ Line 8
    - Ⓓ Line 9

1 Ⓐ Ⓑ Ⓒ Ⓓ   4 Ⓐ Ⓑ Ⓒ Ⓓ   7 Ⓐ Ⓑ Ⓒ Ⓓ   10 Ⓐ Ⓑ Ⓒ Ⓓ
2 Ⓐ Ⓑ Ⓒ Ⓓ   5 Ⓐ Ⓑ Ⓒ Ⓓ   8 Ⓐ Ⓑ Ⓒ Ⓓ   11 Ⓐ Ⓑ Ⓒ Ⓓ
3 Ⓐ Ⓑ Ⓒ Ⓓ   6 Ⓐ Ⓑ Ⓒ Ⓓ   9 Ⓐ Ⓑ Ⓒ Ⓓ   12 Ⓐ Ⓑ Ⓒ Ⓓ

Choose the correct answer to complete the conversations.

13. What are you _____?
   (A) reading
   (B) looking
   (C) read
   (D) look

14. _____ a book about the president.
   (A) I read
   (B) I'm reading
   (C) I watch
   (D) I'm watching

15. Do you _____ biographies?
   (A) reading
   (B) like to
   (C) like to read
   (D) liking

16. Yes. _____ them whenever I can.
   (A) I read
   (B) I'm reading
   (C) I like
   (D) I like to

17. _____ swim?
   (A) You like
   (B) You like to
   (C) You do like to
   (D) Do you like to

18. No. _____ a very good swimmer.
   (A) I don't
   (B) I'm not
   (C) You're
   (D) You aren't

19. _____ exercise?
   (A) You often
   (B) How often you
   (C) How often do you
   (D) Do you how often

20. I exercise _____.
   (A) three times
   (B) three times a week
   (C) three weeks
   (D) every

21. What do you like to do _____?
   (A) in your free time
   (B) in your time
   (C) in your free
   (D) when your free time

22. I like to _____.
   (A) tennis player
   (B) tennis
   (C) playing tennis
   (D) play tennis

13 (A) (B) (C) (D)   16 (A) (B) (C) (D)   19 (A) (B) (C) (D)   21 (A) (B) (C) (D)

14 (A) (B) (C) (D)   17 (A) (B) (C) (D)   20 (A) (B) (C) (D)   22 (A) (B) (C) (D)

15 (A) (B) (C) (D)   18 (A) (B) (C) (D)

Go to the next page ⟶

C CLOZE READING: Grading Systems

Choose the correct answers to complete the paragraph.

There | am is are | different types of grading systems | out in between | 23 different
        (A) (B) ●   (A) (B) (C)

schools. Some schools | use uses using | 24 a letter marking system with the letters A, B, C, D,
                        (A) (B) (C)

| between and for | 25 F. | Other Others Another | 26 schools use the letters E, G, F, and P to
  (A) (B) (C)   (A) (B) (C)

describe students as Excellent, | Grade Get Good | 27, Fair, or | Pretty Popular Poor | 28. Some
                                  (A) (B) (C)   (A) (B) (C)

schools | don't doesn't aren't | 29 use letter grades. They use | number numbers names | 30
          (A) (B) (C)   (A) (B) (C)

such as 75%, 80%, 85% or they don't use grades at all.

D READING: The Education System

Look at the table. Choose the correct answer.

Here is a table that shows the levels of high school and college in the education system in the United States. Notice that we use the same words to describe the levels of students in both parts of the education system. Study the table. Then do Numbers 31 through 34.

HIGH SCHOOL GRADE	LEVEL	YEAR OF COLLEGE
9	Freshman	1
10	Sophomore	2
11	Junior	3
12	Senior	4

31. Carla is a junior in high school. What grade is she in?
    (A) Grade 9.
    (B) Grade 10.
    (C) Grade 11.
    (D) Grade 12.

32. Martin is in his last year as a student at Carleton College. Which sentence is correct?
    (A) He's in Grade 9.
    (B) He's a freshman.
    (C) He's in Grade 12.
    (D) He's a senior.

33. Wendy is a sophomore. She's 20 years old. Which sentence is probably true?
    (A) Wendy goes to high school.
    (B) Wendy goes to college.
    (C) Wendy is in the 10th grade.
    (D) Wendy was a junior last year.

34. The paragraph describes two parts of the education system. What is another part of the education system that isn't described in the paragraph?
    (A) Elementary schools.
    (B) High schools.
    (C) Colleges.
    (D) Supermarkets.

. . . .

23 (A) (B) (C) (D)   26 (A) (B) (C) (D)   29 (A) (B) (C) (D)   32 (A) (B) (C) (D)

24 (A) (B) (C) (D)   27 (A) (B) (C) (D)   30 (A) (B) (C) (D)   33 (A) (B) (C) (D)

25 (A) (B) (C) (D)   28 (A) (B) (C) (D)   31 (A) (B) (C) (D)   34 (A) (B) (C) (D)

Go to the next page ⟶

T3

E. LISTENING ASSESSMENT: An Automated Message

Read and listen to the questions. Then listen to the automated telephone message and answer the questions.

35. How can you listen to the information in Spanish?
    - A Press 1.
    - B Press 2.
    - C Press 3.
    - D Press 4.

36. How can you listen to the information in Arabic?
    - A Press 4.
    - B Press 5.
    - C Press 6.
    - D Press 7.

37. How many days a week is the program open?
    - A Two.
    - B Three.
    - C Five.
    - D Seven.

38. When can you take a placement test for fall English classes?
    - A August 26.
    - B September 3.
    - C September 10.
    - D September 26.

39. On what date do fall classes begin?
    - A September 2.
    - B September 3.
    - C September 10.
    - D 8:30 A.M.

40. How can you listen to the information again?
    - A Press 1.
    - B Press S.
    - C Press #.
    - D Press *.

F. WRITING ASSESSMENT: A Personal Information Form

Name: _____

Address: _____

City: _____ State: _____ Zip Code: _____

Social Security Number: _____ Country of Origin: _____

Telephone: _____ E-mail: _____ Date of Birth: _____

Height: _____ Eye Color: _____ Hair Color: _____ Marital Status: _____

Family Members in Household (Name—Relationship):

_____ _____

_____ _____

G. SPEAKING ASSESSMENT

I can ask and answer these questions:

Ask Answer
- ☐ ☐ Where are you from?
- ☐ ☐ Where do you live now?
- ☐ ☐ Are you married?
- ☐ ☐ Are you single?

Ask Answer
- ☐ ☐ Who are the people in your family?
- ☐ ☐ Do you work or go to school?
- ☐ ☐ What do you do/study?
- ☐ ☐ What do you like to do in your free time?

- -

35 Ⓐ Ⓑ Ⓒ Ⓓ   37 Ⓐ Ⓑ Ⓒ Ⓓ   39 Ⓐ Ⓑ Ⓒ Ⓓ

36 Ⓐ Ⓑ Ⓒ Ⓓ   38 Ⓐ Ⓑ Ⓒ Ⓓ   40 Ⓐ Ⓑ Ⓒ Ⓓ

STOP

A SMALL TALK ABOUT PAST EVENTS

Choose the correct answer.

Example:

My children _____ sick yesterday.
- (A) are
- (B) is
- (C) was
- ● were

1. Traffic _____ very bad this morning.
   - (A) are
   - (B) be
   - (C) was
   - (D) were

2. I _____ a movie last night.
   - (A) go
   - (B) went
   - (C) see
   - (D) saw

3. I _____ sleep well last night.
   - (A) don't
   - (B) didn't
   - (C) am not
   - (D) doesn't

4. Did you _____ today?
   - (A) the bus
   - (B) bus to work
   - (C) take the bus
   - (D) took the bus

5. What _____ last weekend?
   - (A) did you do
   - (B) do you did
   - (C) you do
   - (D) you did

6. Our supervisor _____ very angry this morning.
   - (A) did
   - (B) was
   - (C) be
   - (D) were

7. _____ you nervous while the boss was visiting our department?
   - (A) Are
   - (B) Will
   - (C) Was
   - (D) Were

8. _____ a good vacation?
   - (A) You had
   - (B) Did you had
   - (C) Did you have
   - (D) Had you

9. I _____ an accident while I _____ to work today.
   - (A) see . . . was driving
   - (B) saw . . . was driving
   - (C) saw . . . am driving
   - (D) was seeing . . . drove

1 (A) (B) (C) (D)   4 (A) (B) (C) (D)   7 (A) (B) (C) (D)

2 (A) (B) (C) (D)   5 (A) (B) (C) (D)   8 (A) (B) (C) (D)

3 (A) (B) (C) (D)   6 (A) (B) (C) (D)   9 (A) (B) (C) (D)

Go to the next page ⟩ T5

B GRAMMAR IN CONTEXT: Apologizing & Making Excuses

Choose the correct answer to complete the conversations.

Ex: _____ I arrived late this morning.
- Ⓐ I sorry
- ● I'm sorry
- Ⓒ You sorry
- Ⓓ You're sorry

11. My car _____ while I was driving to work.
- Ⓐ broke down
- Ⓑ break down
- Ⓒ breaks down
- Ⓓ breaking down

13. I want to _____ .
- Ⓐ apology
- Ⓑ apologize
- Ⓒ apologizing
- Ⓓ sorry

15. I _____ finish my work today.
- Ⓐ do
- Ⓑ did
- Ⓒ could
- Ⓓ couldn't

17. I hurt _____ while I was moving some boxes.
- Ⓐ myself
- Ⓑ me
- Ⓒ you
- Ⓓ back

Yes. I'm okay.

10. What _____ ?
- Ⓐ happen
- Ⓑ happens
- Ⓒ happening
- Ⓓ happened

12. _____ bad.
- Ⓐ You
- Ⓑ You're too
- Ⓒ That's too
- Ⓓ That

14. For _____ ?
- Ⓐ what
- Ⓑ when
- Ⓒ why
- Ⓓ how

16. _____ not?
- Ⓐ You're
- Ⓑ Who
- Ⓒ What
- Ⓓ Why

18. _____ to hear that. Are you okay?
- Ⓐ You're sorry
- Ⓑ I'm sorry
- Ⓒ I'm glad
- Ⓓ You're glad

Good.

....

10 Ⓐ Ⓑ Ⓒ Ⓓ   13 Ⓐ Ⓑ Ⓒ Ⓓ   16 Ⓐ Ⓑ Ⓒ Ⓓ

11 Ⓐ Ⓑ Ⓒ Ⓓ   14 Ⓐ Ⓑ Ⓒ Ⓓ   17 Ⓐ Ⓑ Ⓒ Ⓓ

12 Ⓐ Ⓑ Ⓒ Ⓓ   15 Ⓐ Ⓑ Ⓒ Ⓓ   18 Ⓐ Ⓑ Ⓒ Ⓓ

Go to the next page ⟩

C GRAMMAR IN CONTEXT: Oral Directions to Places; Clarification Strategies

Choose the correct answer to complete the conversations.

Ex: Excuse me. _____ the post office?
- Ⓐ Can I get
- Ⓑ Where can I
- Ⓒ How can
- ● How can I get to

19. Walk to the end of this block and _____ right.
- Ⓐ make
- Ⓑ have
- Ⓒ turn
- Ⓓ get

20. Can you tell me _____ Garden Street?
- Ⓐ how to get
- Ⓑ how to get to
- Ⓒ how you go
- Ⓓ how I go

21. Go _____ one block, turn left, and then _____ your second right.
- Ⓐ straight . . . make
- Ⓑ straight . . . turn
- Ⓒ street . . . take
- Ⓓ street . . . turn

22. Straight, left, and then the second _____ ?
- Ⓐ take
- Ⓑ straight
- Ⓒ left
- Ⓓ right

23. Yes. _____
- Ⓐ I'm correct.
- Ⓑ You're wrong.
- Ⓒ That's correct.
- Ⓓ That's incorrect.

24. Take Bus Number 7 and _____ at Lake Street.
- Ⓐ take off
- Ⓑ get on
- Ⓒ get off
- Ⓓ take on

25. _____ Bus Number 11?
- Ⓐ Did you say
- Ⓑ You say
- Ⓒ Do you say
- Ⓓ Did I say

26. _____ Number 7.
- Ⓐ Yes.
- Ⓑ No.
- Ⓒ Maybe.
- Ⓓ You say.

27. And _____ should I get off?
- Ⓐ who
- Ⓑ why
- Ⓒ how
- Ⓓ where

At Lake Street.

Thank you.

19 Ⓐ Ⓑ ⓒ Ⓓ   22 Ⓐ Ⓑ ⓒ Ⓓ   25 Ⓐ Ⓑ ⓒ Ⓓ
20 Ⓐ Ⓑ ⓒ Ⓓ   23 Ⓐ Ⓑ ⓒ Ⓓ   26 Ⓐ Ⓑ ⓒ Ⓓ
21 Ⓐ Ⓑ ⓒ Ⓓ   24 Ⓐ Ⓑ ⓒ Ⓓ   27 Ⓐ Ⓑ ⓒ Ⓓ

Here is part of an accident report that describes an accident between two motor vehicles. Study the diagram and read the statement. Then do Numbers 28 through 31.

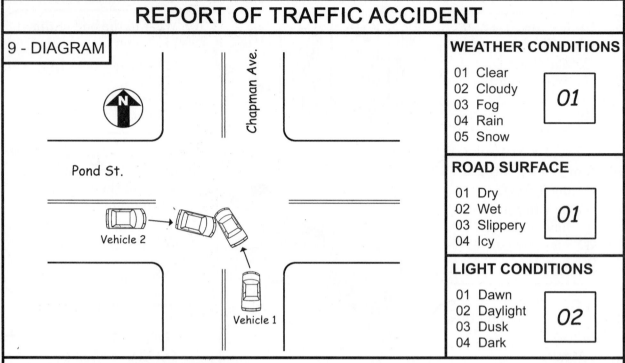

REPORT OF TRAFFIC ACCIDENT

9 - DIAGRAM

Chapman Ave.

Pond St.

Vehicle 2

Vehicle 1

WEATHER CONDITIONS

01 Clear
02 Cloudy
03 Fog
04 Rain
05 Snow

01

ROAD SURFACE

01 Dry
02 Wet
03 Slippery
04 Icy

01

LIGHT CONDITIONS

01 Dawn
02 Daylight
03 Dusk
04 Dark

02

DESCRIBE WHAT HAPPENED:

I was driving north on Chapman Avenue. Vehicle 2 was going east on Pond Street. While I was making a left turn onto Pond Street, the driver of Vehicle 2 didn't stop at the Stop sign and hit the front left side of my car.

28. Where did this accident happen?
   A On Pond Street.
   B On Chapman Avenue.
   C While Vehicle 1 was turning left.
   D At the intersection of Pond and Chapman.

29. Where did Vehicle 2 hit Vehicle 1?
   A At the front right side.
   B At the back right side.
   C At the driver's side in the front.
   D At the driver's side in the back.

30. Where did the driver of Vehicle 1 want to go?
   A West on Pond Street.
   B East on Pond Street.
   C North on Pond Street.
   D South on Chapman Avenue.

31. When the police officer arrived, which driver probably received a ticket for a traffic violation?
   A The driver of Vehicle 1.
   B The driver of Vehicle 2.
   C Both drivers.
   D Neither driver.

28 Ⓐ Ⓑ Ⓒ Ⓓ   30 Ⓐ Ⓑ Ⓒ Ⓓ

29 Ⓐ Ⓑ Ⓒ Ⓓ   31 Ⓐ Ⓑ Ⓒ Ⓓ

Name _____ Date _____

E CLOZE READING: Traffic

Choose the correct answers to complete the story.

I [arrived ● / get Ⓑ / go Ⓒ] at work late yesterday. I usually [drove Ⓐ / drive Ⓑ / went Ⓒ] ³² on the

Jackson Parkway to get to work, but there was bad [cars Ⓐ / slow Ⓑ / traffic Ⓒ] ³³ on the parkway

yesterday. Instead, I [drive Ⓐ / drove Ⓑ / take Ⓒ] ³⁴ to work on Central Avenue. Unfortunately, there

was a bad [accident Ⓐ / traffic Ⓑ / road Ⓒ] ³⁵ on Central Avenue. Traffic [doesn't Ⓐ / didn't Ⓑ / isn't Ⓒ] ³⁶ move

for about an hour [where Ⓐ / who Ⓑ / while Ⓒ] ³⁷ the police helped the people in the accident.

F LISTENING ASSESSMENT: Following Directions to a Place

Read and listen to the questions. Then listen to the telephone conversation and answer the questions.

38. What is Rosa's address?
   Ⓐ 4013 Lake Street.
   Ⓑ 1430 Lake Street.
   Ⓒ 1430 Madison Street.
   Ⓓ 4013 Madison Street.

39. Where is David during this conversation?
   Ⓐ On Bus Number 5.
   Ⓑ At Rosa's party.
   Ⓒ At the post office.
   Ⓓ At an intersection.

40. Why did David get lost?
   Ⓐ He took the wrong bus.
   Ⓑ He got off the bus at the wrong street.
   Ⓒ He walked the wrong way on Lake Street.
   Ⓓ He walked the wrong way on Madison Street.

G LEARNING SKILL: Listing Events in Chronological Order

Put the events in order.

___3___ I worked in my office all morning.
___6___ I went home at 6 P.M.
___5___ I went to a meeting in the afternoon.
___1___ I got dressed and had breakfast.
___4___ I had lunch at noon.
___2___ I took the bus to work.

32 Ⓐ Ⓑ Ⓒ Ⓓ 35 Ⓐ Ⓑ Ⓒ Ⓓ 38 Ⓐ Ⓑ Ⓒ Ⓓ
33 Ⓐ Ⓑ Ⓒ Ⓓ 36 Ⓐ Ⓑ Ⓒ Ⓓ 39 Ⓐ Ⓑ Ⓒ Ⓓ
34 Ⓐ Ⓑ Ⓒ Ⓓ 37 Ⓐ Ⓑ Ⓒ Ⓓ 40 Ⓐ Ⓑ Ⓒ Ⓓ

Imagine that you and another student were in a traffic accident. You were driving Vehicle 1. The other student was driving Vehicle 2. Work together to decide what happened and where. Then work separately to draw a diagram and write a statement about the accident. Finally, exchange information to complete the accident report.

REPORT OF TRAFFIC ACCIDENT

DIAGRAM (Draw a diagram of what happened.)

WEATHER CONDITIONS	ROAD SURFACE	LIGHT CONDITIONS
01 Clear	01 Dry	01 Dawn
02 Cloudy	02 Wet	02 Daylight
03 Fog	03 Slippery	03 Dusk
04 Rain	04 Icy	04 Dark
05 Snow		

DESCRIBE WHAT HAPPENED:

I **SPEAKING ASSESSMENT**

I can ask and answer these questions:

Ask Answer
☐ ☐ What did you do yesterday?
☐ ☐ What did you do last weekend?

Ask Answer
☐ ☐ How did you get to school today?
☐ ☐ How can I get to your home from here?

STOP

Name _____

Date _____ Class _____

3

A COMMUNICATING WITH SCHOOL PERSONNEL

Choose the correct answer.

1. _____ will the parents' meeting start this evening?
   - Ⓐ What day
   - Ⓑ What time
   - Ⓒ What day is it
   - Ⓓ What time is it

2. _____ give this note to my daughter's teacher?
   - Ⓐ You will
   - Ⓑ Please you will
   - Ⓒ You will please
   - Ⓓ Will you please

3. I promise _____ my daughter with her homework.
   - Ⓐ help
   - Ⓑ you help
   - Ⓒ I'll help
   - Ⓓ you'll help

4. _____ school tomorrow?
   - Ⓐ Will there be
   - Ⓑ Will be
   - Ⓒ Will open
   - Ⓓ Will be open

5. Could I _____ a pencil to fill out this form?
   - Ⓐ has
   - Ⓑ give
   - Ⓒ borrow
   - Ⓓ lend

6. Would you _____ me a textbook during the summer so I can help my son with math?
   - Ⓐ take
   - Ⓑ lend
   - Ⓒ read
   - Ⓓ borrow

7. Is Anthony _____ fail math this year?
   - Ⓐ going
   - Ⓑ going to
   - Ⓒ will
   - Ⓓ will be

8. _____ help me fill out this registration form?
   - Ⓐ Could you
   - Ⓑ Could I
   - Ⓒ Will I
   - Ⓓ Would we

9. _____ is my daughter doing in your class?
   - Ⓐ Why
   - Ⓑ When
   - Ⓒ Where
   - Ⓓ How

10. In my _____, the students aren't getting enough homework.
    - Ⓐ think
    - Ⓑ thinks
    - Ⓒ opinion
    - Ⓓ I think

11. My son _____ be in school tomorrow. _____ absent.
    - Ⓐ will . . . He's
    - Ⓑ will . . . He'll be
    - Ⓒ won't . . . He's
    - Ⓓ won't . . . He'll be

12. I think my son _____ doing his homework well because he _____ understand the assignments.
    - Ⓐ is . . . doesn't
    - Ⓑ isn't . . . doesn't
    - Ⓒ is . . . don't
    - Ⓓ isn't . . . does

....

1 Ⓐ Ⓑ Ⓒ Ⓓ   4 Ⓐ Ⓑ Ⓒ Ⓓ   7 Ⓐ Ⓑ Ⓒ Ⓓ   10 Ⓐ Ⓑ Ⓒ Ⓓ

2 Ⓐ Ⓑ Ⓒ Ⓓ   5 Ⓐ Ⓑ Ⓒ Ⓓ   8 Ⓐ Ⓑ Ⓒ Ⓓ   11 Ⓐ Ⓑ Ⓒ Ⓓ

3 Ⓐ Ⓑ Ⓒ Ⓓ   6 Ⓐ Ⓑ Ⓒ Ⓓ   9 Ⓐ Ⓑ Ⓒ Ⓓ   12 Ⓐ Ⓑ Ⓒ Ⓓ

Go to the next page ⟩   **T11**

B GRAMMAR IN CONTEXT: Communicating with School Personnel—Reporting an Absence & Making an Appointment

Choose the correct answer to complete the conversations.

Good morning. Franklin Elementary School.

Yes, Mr. Chen?

15. What's _____ teacher's name?
- (A) my
- (B) your
- (C) her
- (D) his ✓

13. Hello. _____ Peter Chen
- (A) This is ✓
- (B) I
- (C) You
- (D) You are

14. My son, Jason, is sick. He'll be _____ today.
- (A) a clinic
- (B) a doctor
- (C) absent ✓
- (D) present

16. He's in Mrs. Tyler's _____ class.
- (A) four ✓
- (B) fourth grade
- (C) grade
- (D) room

17. Hello. This is Sonia Belkin. I'd like to _____ with the principal.
- (A) make an appointment ✓
- (B) appoint
- (C) appointment
- (D) meeting

19. No. _____ working. How about the day after tomorrow?
- (A) You're
- (B) I
- (C) I'll
- (D) I'll be ✓

21. Can I _____ with him next Monday morning?
- (A) meet ✓
- (B) meeting
- (C) appoint
- (D) appointment

Yes. Thank you.

18. Yes, Mrs. Belkin. Can you _____ tomorrow at 9 A.M.?
- (A) go
- (B) go out
- (C) come in ✓
- (D) appointment

20. I'm sorry. Mr. Price _____ be here. _____ at a meeting.
- (A) will . . . He'll be
- (B) won't . . . He'll be ✓
- (C) will . . . He'll
- (D) won't . . . He'll

22. Yes. _____ 10:00 okay?
- (A) Will
- (B) Be
- (C) Meet
- (D) Is ✓

See you Monday, Mrs. Belkin.

13 (A) (B) (C) (D)	16 (A) (B) (C) (D)	19 (A) (B) (C) (D)	21 (A) (B) (C) (D)
14 (A) (B) (C) (D)	17 (A) (B) (C) (D)	20 (A) (B) (C) (D)	22 (A) (B) (C) (D)
15 (A) (B) (C) (D)	18 (A) (B) (C) (D)		

Go to the next page ▷

C READING: A School Diagram

Here is a diagram of one floor of a high school. Study the diagram. Then do Numbers 23 through 30.

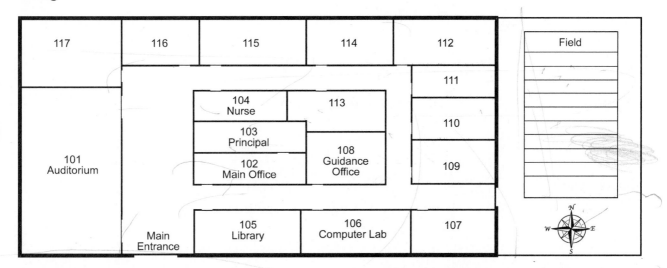

23. What's across from the main office?
    - Ⓐ The gym.
    - Ⓑ The guidance office.
    - Ⓒ The library.
    - Ⓓ The computer lab.

24. The music classroom is behind the auditorium. What's the music teacher's room number?
    - Ⓐ 114.
    - Ⓑ 115.
    - Ⓒ 116.
    - Ⓓ 117.

25. Where is the school's field?
    - Ⓐ On the east side.
    - Ⓑ On the west side.
    - Ⓒ On the south side.
    - Ⓓ On the north side.

26. Irene needs advice about her college applications. Where is she probably going?
    - Ⓐ To Room 102.
    - Ⓑ To Room 105.
    - Ⓒ To Room 106.
    - Ⓓ To Room 108.

27. Carlos doesn't feel well. Where is he probably going?
    - Ⓐ To Room 104.
    - Ⓑ To Room 103.
    - Ⓒ To Room 102.
    - Ⓓ To Room 101.

28. The cafeteria in this school is in Room 10. Where is it probably located?
    - Ⓐ In the auditorium.
    - Ⓑ In the basement.
    - Ⓒ On the first floor.
    - Ⓓ On the second floor.

29. Ms. Martin's classroom is Room Number 233. Where is it probably located?
    - Ⓐ In the basement.
    - Ⓑ On the first floor.
    - Ⓒ On the second floor.
    - Ⓓ On the third floor.

30. Which of these classrooms probably doesn't have any windows?
    - Ⓐ Room 109.
    - Ⓑ Room 111.
    - Ⓒ Room 113.
    - Ⓓ Room 115.

23 Ⓐ Ⓑ Ⓒ Ⓓ   25 Ⓐ Ⓑ Ⓒ Ⓓ   27 Ⓐ Ⓑ Ⓒ Ⓓ   29 Ⓐ Ⓑ Ⓒ Ⓓ

24 Ⓐ Ⓑ Ⓒ Ⓓ   26 Ⓐ Ⓑ Ⓒ Ⓓ   28 Ⓐ Ⓑ Ⓒ Ⓓ   30 Ⓐ Ⓑ Ⓒ Ⓓ

D CLOZE READING: A Note to School

Choose the correct answers to complete the note.

Dare Dear Deer Ms. Watson,
  (A) ● (C)

Your Her My ³¹ daughter, Victoria, won't will not ³² be in school tomorrow
  (A) (B) (C)   (A) (B) (C)

morning. She She'll She's ³³ be at the doctor's office. She have has to has ³⁴ an
           (A) (B) (C)   (A) (B) (C)

appointment at 9:30. I I'll She'll ³⁵ bring her to school during after for ³⁶ the
                     (A) (B) (C)   (A) (B) (C)

appointment.

Sincerely Dear Thank ³⁷,
  (A) (B) (C)

Lydia Petrero

E LISTENING ASSESSMENT: Communicating with School Personnel

Read and listen to the questions. Then listen to the telephone conversation and answer the questions.

38. Who is sick?
   (A) Raymond Vacano.
   (B) Mrs. Vacano.
   (C) The school nurse.
   (D) The gym teacher.

39. Where is the student now?
   (A) At home.
   (B) In the gym.
   (C) In the main office.
   (D) In the nurse's office.

40. Where should the mother go?
   (A) To the gym.
   (B) To the hospital.
   (C) To the nurse's office.
   (D) To the main office.

F WRITING ASSESSMENT: A Note to a Teacher

Write a note to your teacher. Explain why you will be absent during your next English class. (Use a separate sheet of paper.)

G SPEAKING ASSESSMENT: Small Talk about Weekend Plans

I can ask and answer these questions:

Ask Answer
☐ ☐ What are you going to do this Saturday?
☐ ☐ What are you going to do this Sunday?
☐ ☐ What's the weather forecast for the weekend?

....

31 (A)(B)(C)(D)   34 (A)(B)(C)(D)   37 (A)(B)(C)(D)   39 (A)(B)(C)(D)
32 (A)(B)(C)(D)   35 (A)(B)(C)(D)   38 (A)(B)(C)(D)   40 (A)(B)(C)(D)
33 (A)(B)(C)(D)   36 (A)(B)(C)(D)

STOP

T14

A ASKING & ANSWERING TYPICAL JOB INTERVIEW QUESTIONS

Choose the correct answer.

1. Do you know how to _____ a bus?
   - Ⓐ drive
   - Ⓑ drives
   - Ⓒ drove
   - Ⓓ driven

2. I've _____ reports for many years.
   - Ⓐ write
   - Ⓑ writes
   - Ⓒ wrote
   - Ⓓ written

3. Have you ever _____ a presentation?
   - Ⓐ give
   - Ⓑ given
   - Ⓒ gave
   - Ⓓ gives

4. _____ you able to work weekends?
   - Ⓐ Was
   - Ⓑ Do
   - Ⓒ Are
   - Ⓓ Can

5. I know how to _____ inventory.
   - Ⓐ took
   - Ⓑ take
   - Ⓒ taken
   - Ⓓ takes

6. Have you ever _____ arrested?
   - Ⓐ is
   - Ⓑ was
   - Ⓒ be
   - Ⓓ been

7. I can _____ three languages.
   - Ⓐ speak
   - Ⓑ spoke
   - Ⓒ speaks
   - Ⓓ spoken

8. I _____ a computer class last year.
   - Ⓐ take
   - Ⓑ takes
   - Ⓒ took
   - Ⓓ taken

9. What _____ you do in your previous job?
   - Ⓐ do
   - Ⓑ did
   - Ⓒ does
   - Ⓓ done

10. Have you ever _____ a truck?
    - Ⓐ drive
    - Ⓑ drove
    - Ⓒ drives
    - Ⓓ driven

B SMALL TALK ABOUT LEISURE ACTIVITIES

11. A. Have you ever _____ skiing?
    B. Yes. I _____ skiing last year.
    - Ⓐ went . . . go
    - Ⓑ went . . . went
    - Ⓒ gone . . . went
    - Ⓓ go . . . went

12. A. Have you _____ the new Harry Potter movie yet?
    B. Yes. I _____ it last weekend.
    - Ⓐ seen . . . saw
    - Ⓑ saw . . . saw
    - Ⓒ see . . . seen
    - Ⓓ seen . . . see

13. A. I _____ to the mountains last Sunday.
    B. I've never _____ to the mountains.
    - Ⓐ driven . . . drove
    - Ⓑ driven . . . driven
    - Ⓒ drove . . . drove
    - Ⓓ drove . . . driven

14. A. Are you going to _____ today?
    B. No. I've already _____ this week.
    - Ⓐ swim . . . swam
    - Ⓑ swim . . . swum
    - Ⓒ swum . . . swum
    - Ⓓ swam . . . swim

1 Ⓐ Ⓑ Ⓒ Ⓓ   5 Ⓐ Ⓑ Ⓒ Ⓓ   9 Ⓐ Ⓑ Ⓒ Ⓓ   13 Ⓐ Ⓑ Ⓒ Ⓓ

2 Ⓐ Ⓑ Ⓒ Ⓓ   6 Ⓐ Ⓑ Ⓒ Ⓓ   10 Ⓐ Ⓑ Ⓒ Ⓓ   14 Ⓐ Ⓑ Ⓒ Ⓓ

3 Ⓐ Ⓑ Ⓒ Ⓓ   7 Ⓐ Ⓑ Ⓒ Ⓓ   11 Ⓐ Ⓑ Ⓒ Ⓓ

4 Ⓐ Ⓑ Ⓒ Ⓓ   8 Ⓐ Ⓑ Ⓒ Ⓓ   12 Ⓐ Ⓑ Ⓒ Ⓓ

C GRAMMAR IN CONTEXT: Job Interview

15. Do you know how to _____ X-rays?
- Ⓐ take
- Ⓑ takes
- Ⓒ took
- Ⓓ taken

16. Yes. I've _____ X-rays for many years.
- Ⓐ take
- Ⓑ takes
- Ⓒ took
- Ⓓ taken

17. Where _____ you work now?
- Ⓐ does
- Ⓑ do
- Ⓒ done
- Ⓓ did

18. _____ work at the Midtown Clinic.
- Ⓐ I
- Ⓑ I'm
- Ⓒ I've
- Ⓓ I'll

19. _____ you worked there for a long time?
- Ⓐ Do
- Ⓑ Did
- Ⓒ Have
- Ⓓ Has

20. Yes. _____ worked there for many years.
- Ⓐ I
- Ⓑ I'm
- Ⓒ I've
- Ⓓ I did

D GRAMMAR IN CONTEXT: Following a Sequence of Instructions; Organizing Tasks

21. First, _____ the paychecks from the payroll office.
- Ⓐ get
- Ⓑ got
- Ⓒ gets
- Ⓓ gotten

22. I've already _____ them.
- Ⓐ get
- Ⓑ got
- Ⓒ gets
- Ⓓ gotten

23. Then _____ the paychecks to the mailroom.
- Ⓐ took
- Ⓑ take
- Ⓒ taken
- Ⓓ takes

24. I've _____ them there already.
- Ⓐ took
- Ⓑ take
- Ⓒ taken
- Ⓓ takes

25. Finally, _____ the paychecks in each employee's mailbox.
- Ⓐ put
- Ⓑ puts
- Ⓒ have put
- Ⓓ did put

26. I haven't _____ that yet, but I'll _____ it right away.
- Ⓐ do . . . do
- Ⓑ did . . . do
- Ⓒ done . . . do
- Ⓓ done . . . doing

15 Ⓐ Ⓑ Ⓒ Ⓓ   18 Ⓐ Ⓑ Ⓒ Ⓓ   21 Ⓐ Ⓑ Ⓒ Ⓓ   24 Ⓐ Ⓑ Ⓒ Ⓓ

16 Ⓐ Ⓑ Ⓒ Ⓓ   19 Ⓐ Ⓑ Ⓒ Ⓓ   22 Ⓐ Ⓑ Ⓒ Ⓓ   25 Ⓐ Ⓑ Ⓒ Ⓓ

17 Ⓐ Ⓑ Ⓒ Ⓓ   20 Ⓐ Ⓑ Ⓒ Ⓓ   23 Ⓐ Ⓑ Ⓒ Ⓓ   26 Ⓐ Ⓑ Ⓒ Ⓓ

Go to the next page ▷

E CLOZE READING: Employment Application Procedures

Choose the correct answers to complete the story.

I've completed my job [applying (A)] [application (●)] [employer (C)] form. I've filled in all my personal

[application (A)] [vocation (B)] [information (C)✗] 27 I've stated the [position (A)✗] [company (B)] [employee (C)] 28

I'm applying for. I've listed my high school and college in the [work (A)] [education (B)✗] [application (C)] 29

history. I've listed my [now (A)] [today (B)] [current (C)✗] 30 and former jobs. I've written my

[days (A)] [dates (B)✗] [schedules (C)] 31 of employment for each position. I've written the name and address

of each [employer (A)✗] [employee (B)] [employment (C)] 32. I've given the [explain (A)] [excuse (B)] [reason (C)✗] 33 for

leaving each position. I've given the names of three [applications (A)] [references (B)✗] [addresses (C)] 34.

I've described all my [skills (A)✗] [works (B)] [job (C)] 35, including languages I [know (A)✗] [can (B)] [how (C)] 36 speak. I've

[correct (A)] [listed (B)] [checked (C)✗] 37 the application to make sure it is complete.

F LISTENING ASSESSMENT: A Job Interview

Read and listen to the questions. Then listen to the job interview and answer the questions.

38. Where is the job interview probably taking place?
    - (A) At a supermarket.
    - (B) In a restaurant.
    - (C) At a school.
    - (D)✗ In a department store.

39. When CAN'T the job applicant work?
    - (A)✗ Mornings
    - (B) Afternoons.
    - (C) Evenings.
    - (D) Weekends.

40. How often are the employees paid?
    - (A) Once a year.
    - (B) Once a month.
    - (C)✗ Once a week.
    - (D) Once a day.

27 (A) (B) (C) (D) 31 (A) (B) (C) (D) 35 (A) (B) (C) (D) 39 (A) (B) (C) (D)
28 (A) (B) (C) (D) 32 (A) (B) (C) (D) 36 (A) (B) (C) (D) 40 (A) (B) (C) (D)
29 (A) (B) (C) (D) 33 (A) (B) (C) (D) 37 (A) (B) (C) (D)
30 (A) (B) (C) (D) 34 (A) (B) (C) (D) 38 (A) (B) (C) (D)

Go to the next page T17

Complete the job application form. (Use any information you wish.)

PERSONAL INFORMATION

NAME _____ SOCIAL SECURITY NUMBER _____
     LAST   FIRST   MIDDLE

ADDRESS _____ TELEPHONE _____
     NUMBER STREET   CITY   STATE   ZIP CODE

EDUCATION HISTORY

HIGH SCHOOL _____ DIPLOMA OR GED RECEIVED: __ YES __ NO DATE _____
     NAME   CITY   STATE

COLLEGE/VOCATIONAL SCHOOL

NAME	LOCATION	FIELD OF STUDY	DEGREE/CERTIFICATION	DATE

EMPLOYMENT HISTORY (List most recent first.)

Date	Name & Address of Employer	Position	Salary	Name of Supervisor	Reason for Leaving
From: To:					
Duties					
From: To:					
Duties					
From: To:					
Duties					

SKILLS

LIST ANY SPECIAL TRAINING OR SKILLS YOU HAVE

_____

_____

SIGNATURE _____ DATE _____

I can ask and answer these questions:

Ask Answer

☐ ☐ Do you know how to _____?

☐ ☐ Have you seen *title of movie* ?

Ask Answer

☐ ☐ What have you already done today?

☐ ☐ What haven't you done yet?

STOP

A GIVING PERSONAL INFORMATION ABOUT SELF, FAMILY, & JOB HISTORY

Example:

How long have you _____ a mechanic?
- Ⓐ are
- Ⓑ were
- Ⓒ be
- ⬤ been

1. Have you always _____ here in Miami?
   - Ⓐ live
   - Ⓑ lived
   - Ⓒ living
   - Ⓓ you lived

2. How long have you _____ how to fix computers?
   - Ⓐ know
   - Ⓑ knew
   - Ⓒ known
   - Ⓓ knows

3. I've been a taxi driver _____ three years.
   - Ⓐ for
   - Ⓑ since
   - Ⓒ during
   - Ⓓ with

4. My family has lived here _____ 2001.
   - Ⓐ until
   - Ⓑ since
   - Ⓒ before
   - Ⓓ for

5. I've known how to speak French _____ a child.
   - Ⓐ for I'm
   - Ⓑ for I was
   - Ⓒ since I'm
   - Ⓓ since I was

6. Have you been a carpenter _____ a long time?
   - Ⓐ for
   - Ⓑ when
   - Ⓒ ago
   - Ⓓ since

7. _____ worked in my current job since May. Before that, _____ worked at a supermarket.
   - Ⓐ I . . . I
   - Ⓑ I . . . I've
   - Ⓒ I've . . . I
   - Ⓓ I've . . . I've

B STATING SKILLS, QUALIFICATIONS, & PERSONAL QUALITIES

Example:

I _____ type, file, and use a computer.
- Ⓐ known how
- Ⓑ known how to
- Ⓒ know how
- ⬤ know how to

8. I _____.
   - Ⓐ hard work
   - Ⓑ harder work
   - Ⓒ work hard
   - Ⓓ am hard work

9. I have a lot of _____.
   - Ⓐ experience
   - Ⓑ employment
   - Ⓒ qualification
   - Ⓓ job

10. I'm never late. I'm very _____.
   - Ⓐ on time
   - Ⓑ for work
   - Ⓒ out of time
   - Ⓓ punctual

1 Ⓐ Ⓑ Ⓒ Ⓓ   4 Ⓐ Ⓑ Ⓒ Ⓓ   7 Ⓐ Ⓑ Ⓒ Ⓓ   9 Ⓐ Ⓑ Ⓒ Ⓓ

2 Ⓐ Ⓑ Ⓒ Ⓓ   5 Ⓐ Ⓑ Ⓒ Ⓓ   8 Ⓐ Ⓑ Ⓒ Ⓓ   10 Ⓐ Ⓑ Ⓒ Ⓓ

3 Ⓐ Ⓑ Ⓒ Ⓓ   6 Ⓐ Ⓑ Ⓒ Ⓓ

Go to the next page ⟶

Example:

_____ you working now?
- (A) Will
- ● Are
- (C) Have
- (D) Do

11. Yes, I _____.
- (A) do
- (B) can
- (C) am
- (D) will

12. Where _____ you work now?
- (A) have
- (B) is
- (C) did
- (D) do

13. _____ at Tops Office Supplies.
- (A) I work
- (B) I worked
- (C) I've worked
- (D) I'll work

14. How long _____ there?
- (A) do you work
- (B) have you worked
- (C) did you work
- (D) does your work

15. _____ there since January.
- (A) I work
- (B) I worked
- (C) I've worked
- (D) I'll work

16. Where _____ before that?
- (A) did you work
- (B) have worked
- (C) do you work
- (D) you work

17. _____ at Shay's Supermarket.
- (A) I work
- (B) I'll work
- (C) I've worked
- (D) I worked

18. How long _____ there?
- (A) you work
- (B) do you work
- (C) did you work
- (D) have you worked

19. _____ two years.
- (A) From
- (B) For
- (C) During
- (D) Since

11 (A) (B) (C) (D)   14 (A) (B) (C) (D)   16 (A) (B) (C) (D)   18 (A) (B) (C) (D)

12 (A) (B) (C) (D)   15 (A) (B) (C) (D)   17 (A) (B) (C) (D)   19 (A) (B) (C) (D)

13 (A) (B) (C) (D)

Go to the next page ⟹

D GRAMMAR IN CONTEXT: Clarifying to Ask for Meaning

Example:
How long have you _____ unemployed?
- Ⓐ be
- ● been
- Ⓒ are
- Ⓓ was

20. I'm sorry. _____ does "unemployed" mean?
- Ⓐ Who
- Ⓑ What
- Ⓒ How
- Ⓓ Why

21. How long _____ out of work?
- Ⓐ you are
- Ⓑ you were
- Ⓒ have you been
- Ⓓ you have been

22. _____ two months.
- Ⓐ For
- Ⓑ Since
- Ⓒ With
- Ⓓ From

23. _____ you naturalized?
- Ⓐ Has
- Ⓑ Did
- Ⓒ Do
- Ⓓ Are

24. I'm sorry. What does that _____?
- Ⓐ say
- Ⓑ word
- Ⓒ mean
- Ⓓ understand

25. _____ you become a citizen yet?
- Ⓐ Do
- Ⓑ Are
- Ⓒ Has
- Ⓓ Have

26. Yes. _____ a citizen since 2003.
- Ⓐ I was
- Ⓑ I've been
- Ⓒ I'm not
- Ⓓ I have

27. _____ you ever been incarcerated?
- Ⓐ Have
- Ⓑ Did
- Ⓒ Were
- Ⓓ Was

28. I'm sorry. I don't _____ what that means.
- Ⓐ ask
- Ⓑ repeat
- Ⓒ understand
- Ⓓ sorry

Have you ever been in jail?

No, I haven't.

20 Ⓐ Ⓑ Ⓒ Ⓓ   23 Ⓐ Ⓑ Ⓒ Ⓓ   25 Ⓐ Ⓑ Ⓒ Ⓓ   27 Ⓐ Ⓑ Ⓒ Ⓓ
21 Ⓐ Ⓑ Ⓒ Ⓓ   24 Ⓐ Ⓑ Ⓒ Ⓓ   26 Ⓐ Ⓑ Ⓒ Ⓓ   28 Ⓐ Ⓑ Ⓒ Ⓓ
22 Ⓐ Ⓑ Ⓒ Ⓓ

E READING: Job Ads

Look at the job advertisements. Then do Numbers 29 through 32.

SaveMart is now hiring!

- Full Time, Part Time, & Sunday Only Positions
- Flexible Hours & Schedules
- Excellent Salary & Benefits
- Store Employee Discount

Positions now available:

Sales • Cashiers • Security

Ask for an application at the Service Desk.

★ Join the BURGER WORLD TEAM!

- FREE MEALS
- FREE UNIFORMS
- PROMOTION OPPORTUNITIES
- REGULAR WAGE INCREASES
- ACADEMIC SCHOLARSHIPS

Counter, Crew, & Manager positions available

CARPENTER
Exper. req. Must have tools & trans. Call 564-9234.

DATA ENTRY CLERK
FT. Will train. Good math skills req. $8/hr. Call 729-4444.

OFFICE ASST.
PT. M–F. 9am–1pm. Office exper. pref. Call 426-8080.

---

29. Which job advertisement isn't in the newspaper?
- A The ad for a carpenter.
- B The ad for cashiers.
- C The ad for an office assistant.
- D The ad for a data entry clerk.

30. Which ad gives the best information about the salary?
- A The ad for a salesperson.
- B The ad for an office assistant.
- C The ad for a carpenter.
- D The ad for a data entry clerk.

31. Which statement about the office assistant position is NOT true?
- A The position is part-time.
- B The person will work 5 days a week.
- C Experience is required.
- D The person will work 20 hours a week.

32. Brenda already works full-time Monday through Friday. She wants to earn more money on weekends. Which job should she apply for?
- A A job at SaveMart.
- B A job at Burger World.
- C The data entry clerk position.
- D The office assistant position.

29 Ⓐ Ⓑ Ⓒ Ⓓ   30 Ⓐ Ⓑ Ⓒ Ⓓ   31 Ⓐ Ⓑ Ⓒ Ⓓ   32 Ⓐ Ⓑ Ⓒ Ⓓ

Go to the next page

T22

Name _____ Date _____

F GRAMMAR IN CONTEXT: Small Talk

Example:
_____ been?
- Ⓐ Are you
- Ⓑ How
- ⬤ How have you
- Ⓓ How you have

33. _____ fine, thanks.
- Ⓐ I've been
- Ⓑ You've been
- Ⓒ You're
- Ⓓ I

34. How long _____ your daughter lived in Portland?
- Ⓐ is
- Ⓑ has
- Ⓒ was
- Ⓓ did

35. She's lived there _____ two years.
- Ⓐ since
- Ⓑ during
- Ⓒ in
- Ⓓ for

36. How long _____ your wife?
- Ⓐ you know
- Ⓑ you knew
- Ⓒ has
- Ⓓ have you known

37. I've known her since _____ in high school.
- Ⓐ we were
- Ⓑ we are
- Ⓒ we're
- Ⓓ she's

G LISTENING ASSESSMENT: Responding to a Job Ad; Abbreviations

Read and listen to the questions. Then listen to the conversation and answer the questions.

38. Which abbreviation describes the hours for this position?
- Ⓐ PT
- Ⓑ FT
- Ⓒ Flexible hrs.
- Ⓓ 8 hrs./wk.

39. Which statement describes the experience this job requires?
- Ⓐ Excel. benefits
- Ⓑ Typing skills pref.
- Ⓒ Office exper. req.
- Ⓓ Office exper. pref.

40. Which sentence is probably in the ad for this job?
- Ⓐ No calls.
- Ⓑ Apply in person.
- Ⓒ Call Pat at 421-2000.
- Ⓓ Ask for Pat at the service counter.

33 Ⓐ Ⓑ Ⓒ Ⓓ   35 Ⓐ Ⓑ Ⓒ Ⓓ   37 Ⓐ Ⓑ Ⓒ Ⓓ   39 Ⓐ Ⓑ Ⓒ Ⓓ
34 Ⓐ Ⓑ Ⓒ Ⓓ   36 Ⓐ Ⓑ Ⓒ Ⓓ   38 Ⓐ Ⓑ Ⓒ Ⓓ   40 Ⓐ Ⓑ Ⓒ Ⓓ

WRITING ASSESSMENT: A Resume

Write a resume. List your work experience, your education history, and your skills (languages you speak, computer skills, machines you can operate, licenses you have).

_____
(Name)

_____
(Address)

_____
(Phone Number or E-mail)

WORK EXPERIENCE (LIST MOST RECENT FIRST)

Dates _____   _____
                    Position, Place of Employment

                    _____
                    City, State

                    _____
                    Description of job duties

Dates _____   _____
                    Position, Place of Employment

                    _____
                    City, State

                    _____
                    Description of job duties

Dates _____   _____
                    Position, Place of Employment

                    _____
                    City, State

                    _____
                    Description of job duties

EDUCATION HISTORY

Dates _____   _____
                    Degree or certificate

                    _____
                    School, City, State

Dates _____   _____
                    Degree or certificate

                    _____
                    School, City, State

SKILLS

_____

_____

I **SPEAKING ASSESSMENT**

I can ask and answer these questions:

Ask Answer

☐ ☐ Where do you live now?
☐ ☐ How long have you lived there?
☐ ☐ Where did you live before that?
☐ ☐ How long did you live there?

Ask Answer

☐ ☐ Who is your best friend?
☐ ☐ How long have you known her/him?
☐ ☐ Who is the leader of your country?
☐ ☐ How long has she/he been the leader?

STOP

A RENTING AN APARTMENT

Example:

How much is the ____?
- ● rent
- Ⓑ landlord
- Ⓒ utilities
- Ⓓ tenant

1. A rental agreement is ____.
   - Ⓐ a landlord
   - Ⓑ a lease
   - Ⓒ a utility
   - Ⓓ rent

2. Are pets ____ in the building?
   - Ⓐ permitted
   - Ⓑ permission
   - Ⓒ may I
   - Ⓓ rules

3. ____ utilities included in the rent?
   - Ⓐ Do
   - Ⓑ Does
   - Ⓒ Are
   - Ⓓ Is

4. What are the ____ of the building?
   - Ⓐ don't
   - Ⓑ allowed
   - Ⓒ permitted
   - Ⓓ rules

5. Does the rent ____ a parking space?
   - Ⓐ include
   - Ⓑ allowed
   - Ⓒ have
   - Ⓓ garage

6. Throw trash in the ____.
   - Ⓐ hallway
   - Ⓑ dumpster
   - Ⓒ recycling bin
   - Ⓓ garbage disposal

7. If something is broken, fill out a ____ request form.
   - Ⓐ pest control
   - Ⓑ problem
   - Ⓒ maintenance
   - Ⓓ building

8. It is prohibited to hang laundry on the ____.
   - Ⓐ entrance
   - Ⓑ apartment
   - Ⓒ balcony
   - Ⓓ place

9. Make sure you understand a lease before you ____ it.
   - Ⓐ deposit
   - Ⓑ write
   - Ⓒ rent
   - Ⓓ sign

1 Ⓐ Ⓑ Ⓒ Ⓓ   4 Ⓐ Ⓑ Ⓒ Ⓓ   7 Ⓐ Ⓑ Ⓒ Ⓓ

2 Ⓐ Ⓑ Ⓒ Ⓓ   5 Ⓐ Ⓑ Ⓒ Ⓓ   8 Ⓐ Ⓑ Ⓒ Ⓓ

3 Ⓐ Ⓑ Ⓒ Ⓓ   6 Ⓐ Ⓑ Ⓒ Ⓓ   9 Ⓐ Ⓑ Ⓒ Ⓓ

Go to the next page ⇒   **T25**

Example:

You _____ tired.
- ● look
- Ⓑ looks
- Ⓒ looking
- Ⓓ looked

10. I am. _____ washing windows since 9:00 this morning.
- Ⓐ I
- Ⓑ I've been
- Ⓒ I'm
- Ⓓ I'll

11. Really? How many windows _____?
- Ⓐ you wash
- Ⓑ you washed
- Ⓒ you have washed
- Ⓓ have you washed

12. _____ eight windows.
- Ⓐ I wash
- Ⓑ I'll wash
- Ⓒ I've washed
- Ⓓ you washed

13. Would you like me to _____?
- Ⓐ help you
- Ⓑ you help
- Ⓒ your help
- Ⓓ help me

14. Thanks. I _____.
- Ⓐ appreciate
- Ⓑ appreciate it
- Ⓒ thank
- Ⓓ grateful

15. What _____ doing?
- Ⓐ you been
- Ⓑ have been
- Ⓒ have you been
- Ⓓ you have been

16. _____ the closets.
- Ⓐ Clean
- Ⓑ I clean
- Ⓒ I'm going to clean
- Ⓓ I've been cleaning

17. _____ I can do to help?
- Ⓐ There's anything
- Ⓑ There's something
- Ⓒ Is anything there
- Ⓓ Is there anything

18. Yes. Please _____ these newspapers in the recycling bin.
- Ⓐ put
- Ⓑ will put
- Ⓒ have put
- Ⓓ you put

10 Ⓐ Ⓑ Ⓒ Ⓓ   13 Ⓐ Ⓑ Ⓒ Ⓓ   15 Ⓐ Ⓑ Ⓒ Ⓓ   17 Ⓐ Ⓑ Ⓒ Ⓓ

11 Ⓐ Ⓑ Ⓒ Ⓓ   14 Ⓐ Ⓑ Ⓒ Ⓓ   16 Ⓐ Ⓑ Ⓒ Ⓓ   18 Ⓐ Ⓑ Ⓒ Ⓓ

12 Ⓐ Ⓑ Ⓒ Ⓓ

Go to the next page ⟹

C READING: Scanning a Utility Bill for Most Essential Information

Look at the utility bill. Then do Numbers 19 through 22.

California Power and Light
P.O. Box 3566
Los Angeles, CA 90016
Web address: www.cpl.com

Customer assistance line
1-800-555-7600
To report a power outage
1-800-555-3000

Account Number **235-12-55-78304**
Hector Nieves
15 Park Drive
Los Angeles, CA 90020

Billing Date: 11/15/10
Payment Due: 12/10/10
Next Meter Read Date: 12/14/10

Billing Summary

Amount of Previous Statement 10/15/10	$ 89.91
Payment Received— 11/09/10 Thank You	89.91
Balance Before Current Charges	0.00
Current Charges	96.45
Your Total Balance Due	$ 96.45

Your current energy usage

Meter Number	From	To	Usage
AB910731	10/14/10	11/14/10	
	51291	51905	614 kilowatt hours

Reminder — a 9% late payment will be added to the total unpaid balance of your account if a full payment is not received by the due date on this bill.

Please write your account number on your check.

19. This is _____.
    Ⓐ a telephone bill
    Ⓑ an electric bill
    Ⓒ a gas bill
    Ⓓ a cable TV bill

20. Mr. Nieves has to pay this bill on or before _____.
    Ⓐ November 14
    Ⓑ November 15
    Ⓒ December 10
    Ⓓ December 14

21. The total amount due now is _____.
    Ⓐ 614 kilowatt hours
    Ⓑ $0.00
    Ⓒ $89.91
    Ⓓ $96.45

22. When Mr. Nieves pays this bill, he should write the number _____ on the check.
    Ⓐ 235-12-55-78304
    Ⓑ 1-800-555-7600
    Ⓒ 1-800-555-3000
    Ⓓ AB910731

19 Ⓐ Ⓑ Ⓒ Ⓓ   20 Ⓐ Ⓑ Ⓒ Ⓓ   21 Ⓐ Ⓑ Ⓒ Ⓓ   22 Ⓐ Ⓑ Ⓒ Ⓓ

Look at the yellow pages listings. Then do Numbers 23 through 26.

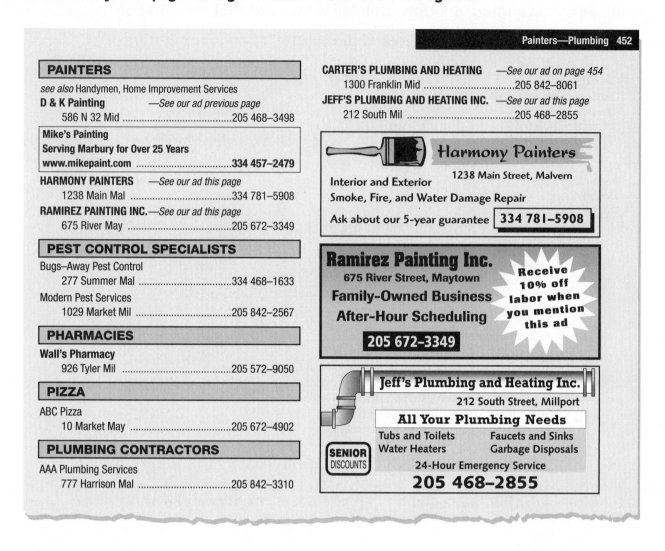

Painters—Plumbing 452

PAINTERS

see also Handymen, Home Improvement Services

D & K Painting —See our ad previous page
586 N 32 Mid 205 468–3498

Mike's Painting
Serving Marbury for Over 25 Years
www.mikepaint.com **334 457–2479**

HARMONY PAINTERS —See our ad this page
1238 Main Mal 334 781–5908

RAMIREZ PAINTING INC.—See our ad this page
675 River May 205 672–3349

PEST CONTROL SPECIALISTS

Bugs–Away Pest Control
277 Summer Mal 334 468–1633

Modern Pest Services
1029 Market Mil 205 842–2567

PHARMACIES

Wall's Pharmacy
926 Tyler Mil 205 572–9050

PIZZA

ABC Pizza
10 Market May 205 672–4902

PLUMBING CONTRACTORS

AAA Plumbing Services
777 Harrison Mal 205 842–3310

CARTER'S PLUMBING AND HEATING —See our ad on page 454
1300 Franklin Mid 205 842–8061

JEFF'S PLUMBING AND HEATING INC. —See our ad this page
212 South Mil 205 468–2855

Harmony Painters
1238 Main Street, Malvern
Interior and Exterior
Smoke, Fire, and Water Damage Repair
Ask about our 5-year guarantee **334 781–5908**

Ramirez Painting Inc.
675 River Street, Maytown
Family-Owned Business
After-Hour Scheduling
205 672–3349
Receive 10% off labor when you mention this ad

Jeff's Plumbing and Heating Inc.
212 South Street, Millport
All Your Plumbing Needs
Tubs and Toilets   Faucets and Sinks
Water Heaters   Garbage Disposals
SENIOR DISCOUNTS
24-Hour Emergency Service
205 468–2855

---

23. You're looking for a painting company in Midfield. You should call _____.
Ⓐ 334 457-2479
Ⓑ 334 781-5908
Ⓒ 205 468-3498
Ⓓ 205 672-3349

24. There are roaches in your kitchen. You live in Malvern. You should call _____.
Ⓐ 334 457-2479
Ⓑ 334 468-1633
Ⓒ 205 842-2567
Ⓓ 205 572-9050

25. It's midnight. A pipe in your bathroom just broke. You should call _____.
Ⓐ 205 468-2855
Ⓑ 205 842-3310
Ⓒ 205 842-8061
Ⓓ 911

26. There isn't an ad for _____ on this page.
Ⓐ Harmony Painters
Ⓑ Jeff's Plumbing and Heating
Ⓒ Ramirez Painting
Ⓓ D & K Painting

....

23 Ⓐ Ⓑ Ⓒ Ⓓ   24 Ⓐ Ⓑ Ⓒ Ⓓ   25 Ⓐ Ⓑ Ⓒ Ⓓ   26 Ⓐ Ⓑ Ⓒ Ⓓ

Go to the next page ⟹

E CLOZE READING: Housing Maintenance & Repairs

Choose the correct answers to complete the notice to tenants in an apartment building.

To: All Tenants
From: Your Building   Maintenance   Mandatory   **Manager**
                          (A)   (B)   ●

Please remember to follow these   reports   rules   requests   27 of the building:
                                    (A)   (B)   (C)

Throw all trash in the   recycling bin   dumpster   hallway   28.
                            (A)   (B)   (C)

Put metal cans and   garbage   landfill   glass   29 in the recycling bins.
                       (A)   (B)   (C)

Don't forget: Recycling in our city is   mandatory   waste   routine   30.
                                            (A)   (B)   (C)

Always turn on the water when you use the garbage   storage   disposal   bin   31.
                                                      (A)   (B)   (C)

Report any broken   pest   kitchen   smoke   32 detectors immediately.
                     (A)   (B)   (C)

Also report any other fire   safety   hazards   service   33.
                              (A)   (B)   (C)

Call the   rental   storage   common   34 office if you need the pest   collection   control   preparation   35
            (A)   (B)   (C)   (A)   (B)   (C)

company.

Please do not call us with routine   maintenance   emergency   request   36 problems.
                                        (A)   (B)   (C)

Fill out a maintenance request   program   law   form   37.
                                   (A)   (B)   (C)

F LISTENING ASSESSMENT: Renting an Apartment

Read and listen to the questions. Then listen to the conversation and answer the questions.

38. Which pets are NOT allowed in the building?
    (A) Birds.
    (B) Small dogs.
    (C) Cats.
    (D) Large dogs.

39. Which utility is included in the rent?
    (A) Electricity.
    (B) Heat.
    (C) Cable TV.
    (D) Telephone.

40. Where can tenants park a second car?
    (A) In the parking lot.
    (B) In the garage.
    (C) In the rental office.
    (D) In the visitor parking spaces.

....

27 (A) (B) (C) (D)   31 (A) (B) (C) (D)   35 (A) (B) (C) (D)   39 (A) (B) (C) (D)

28 (A) (B) (C) (D)   32 (A) (B) (C) (D)   36 (A) (B) (C) (D)   40 (A) (B) (C) (D)

29 (A) (B) (C) (D)   33 (A) (B) (C) (D)   37 (A) (B) (C) (D)

30 (A) (B) (C) (D)   34 (A) (B) (C) (D)   38 (A) (B) (C) (D)   Go to the next page ⟩

WRITING ASSESSMENT: Bank Transactions

Withdraw $200.00 from your savings account. Your account number is 83219745.

Deposit your paycheck for $575.25 in your account and get $100.00 in cash. Your account number is 42439182.

WITHDRAWAL APPLICATION	Date _____

CASH WITHDRAWAL	
CHECK WITHDRAWAL	
TOTAL WITHDRAWAL	

Account number _____

Signature _____

DEPOSIT SLIP	Date _____

CURRENCY	
COIN	
CHECKS	
LESS CASH	
TOTAL	

Account number _____

Name _____

Sign here ONLY if cash received from deposit _____

Fill out the check to pay this bill.

E-Star Energy

Electricity	$37.92
Past Due	0.00
DUE NOW	$37.92

1024

Pay to the
order of _____ $ _____

_____ Dollars

For _____   _____

057009345 200042534 1024

Now record this check in the check register and calculate the new balance.

Number	Date	Description	Amount of Debit (−)	Amount of Credit (+)	Balance
1022	1/14	Metrovision Cable TV	49.50		1,461.50
1023	1/16	Telecom	32.51		1,428.99

H **SPEAKING ASSESSMENT**

I can ask and answer these questions:

Ask Answer
☐ ☐ What street do you live on?
☐ ☐ How long have you been living on that street?
☐ ☐ Where else have you lived?

Ask Answer
☐ ☐ How long have you been studying English?
☐ ☐ Have you ever had a maintenance or repair problem where you live? What happened?

A REQUESTS AT WORK

Example:

Thank you _____ copying the report.
- Ⓐ with
- Ⓑ at
- Ⓒ the
- ● for

1. _____ clean the tables?
   - Ⓐ Please you would
   - Ⓑ Would please you
   - Ⓒ Would you please
   - Ⓓ Please would

2. Could I possibly _____ your pen?
   - Ⓐ lend
   - Ⓑ borrow
   - Ⓒ lend me
   - Ⓓ borrow you

3. Would you please _____ your calculator?
   - Ⓐ borrow
   - Ⓑ borrow me
   - Ⓒ lend
   - Ⓓ lend me

4. _____ happy to do it.
   - Ⓐ I
   - Ⓑ I be
   - Ⓒ I'll be
   - Ⓓ You

5. Thank you for _____ the chairs.
   - Ⓐ setting up
   - Ⓑ sets up
   - Ⓒ set up
   - Ⓓ you set up

6. _____ take the day off tomorrow?
   - Ⓐ I'm possibly
   - Ⓑ Could I possibly
   - Ⓒ I could possibly
   - Ⓓ Could possibly

7. Would you _____ help me with my presentation?
   - Ⓐ possible
   - Ⓑ can
   - Ⓒ are able to
   - Ⓓ be able to

8. I _____ take my son to a doctor's appointment tomorrow.
   - Ⓐ have
   - Ⓑ have to
   - Ⓒ going
   - Ⓓ going to

9. I'm asking for _____ tomorrow because my husband will be in the hospital.
   - Ⓐ the day off
   - Ⓑ the off day
   - Ⓒ day off
   - Ⓓ off day

....

1 Ⓐ Ⓑ Ⓒ Ⓓ   4 Ⓐ Ⓑ Ⓒ Ⓓ   7 Ⓐ Ⓑ Ⓒ Ⓓ

2 Ⓐ Ⓑ Ⓒ Ⓓ   5 Ⓐ Ⓑ Ⓒ Ⓓ   8 Ⓐ Ⓑ Ⓒ Ⓓ

3 Ⓐ Ⓑ Ⓒ Ⓓ   6 Ⓐ Ⓑ Ⓒ Ⓓ   9 Ⓐ Ⓑ Ⓒ Ⓓ

B GRAMMAR IN CONTEXT: Requests at Work; Small Talk at Work

Example:
_____ set up the tables and chairs?
- (A) Please
- (B) You please
- (C) ● Would you please
- (D) You would please

10. _____ be happy to.
- (A) I
- (B) I'll
- (C) You
- (D) You'll

11. Could I possibly _____ a screwdriver?
- (A) borrow
- (B) borrow you
- (C) lend
- (D) lend me

12. _____ Here you are.
- (A) No.
- (B) I'll be happy to.
- (C) You'll be happy to.
- (D) Sure.

13. Thank you _____ your cell phone.
- (A) for borrowing
- (B) for lending you
- (C) for lending me
- (D) please lend me

14. _____ welcome.
- (A) You
- (B) Your
- (C) You're
- (D) I'm

15. _____ was your weekend?
- (A) Who
- (B) What
- (C) Where
- (D) How

16. _____ was great.
- (A) I
- (B) It
- (C) You
- (D) We

17. What _____?
- (A) you do
- (B) did you
- (C) you did
- (D) did you do

18. We _____ to the beach.
- (A) went
- (B) go
- (C) going
- (D) gone

10 (A) (B) (C) (D)   13 (A) (B) (C) (D)   15 (A) (B) (C) (D)   17 (A) (B) (C) (D)
11 (A) (B) (C) (D)   14 (A) (B) (C) (D)   16 (A) (B) (C) (D)   18 (A) (B) (C) (D)
12 (A) (B) (C) (D)

Go to the next page ⟩

C READING: Workplace Notes & Messages

Look at the notes and messages. Then do Numbers 19 through 22.

BizNet

Mr. Lu,
    I'm sorry I was late this morning. My children's school bus didn't come this morning so I had to drive them to school. I'm writing my monthly report and will give it to you by the end of the day.

                    Thanks,
                    Gary

From the desk of
Wanda Torres

Alice,
    Thank you for buying the pizza and soda for yesterday's office party. Everything was great, and all the employees enjoyed themselves. Please give me your receipts as soon as you can and I'll reimburse you.

                    Wanda

From: Dawn_Kendall@BizNet.com
To: Berta_Molina@BizNet.com
Subject: New employee

Berta,
Our new office assistant, Luis Rodriguez, will begin work next Monday. Unfortunately, I won't be here that day because I have some meetings out of town. Could you please show Luis around the office and introduce him to all the employees? Also, please show him how to use the telephone system and bring him to the personnel office so he can get the new employee manual and fill out a W-4 form. Luis can spend the rest of the day reading last year's company report. I'll meet with him on Tuesday morning and talk with him about his job responsibilities.
Thanks very much,
Dawn

---

19. Next Monday, Luis Rodriguez WON'T
    _____.
    Ⓐ fill out a W-4 form
    Ⓑ meet his co-workers
    Ⓒ meet with Dawn Kendall
    Ⓓ begin work at the company

20. An employee is apologizing for something in _____ of these notes and messages.
    Ⓐ three
    Ⓑ two
    Ⓒ one
    Ⓓ none

21. In the note from Wanda to Alice, *reimburse* means _____.
    Ⓐ Alice will give Wanda money
    Ⓑ Wanda will give Alice money
    Ⓒ Alice's salary will be higher
    Ⓓ Wanda will buy the pizza and soda next time

22. We can infer from these notes and messages that _____.
    Ⓐ Alice is Wanda's supervisor
    Ⓑ Luis is Berta's new supervisor
    Ⓒ Luis is Dawn's new supervisor
    Ⓓ Mr. Lu is Gary's supervisor

....

19 Ⓐ Ⓑ Ⓒ Ⓓ   20 Ⓐ Ⓑ Ⓒ Ⓓ   21 Ⓐ Ⓑ Ⓒ Ⓓ   22 Ⓐ Ⓑ Ⓒ Ⓓ

Look at the paycheck and pay stub. Then do Numbers 23 through 28.

TECHNOFILE CORPORATION
PAY PERIOD
04/30/09 – 05/06/09

HADDAD F.

EMP. NO. 46803
PAY DATE:
05/11/09

EARNINGS	RATE	HOURS	THIS PERIOD	YEAR TO DATE
REGULAR	16.00	35	560.00	7,280.00
OVERTIME	24.00	3	72.00	2,232.00
HOLIDAY	32.00	0	0.00	672.00
GROSS PAY			632.00	10,184.00

	THIS PERIOD	YEAR TO DATE	GROSS PAY	632.00
FED TAX	94.80	1,527.60	TAXES	170.64
FICA/MEDICARE	44.24	712.88	OTHER DEDUCTIONS	40.25
STATE TAX	31.60	509.20		
HEALTH	40.25	523.25	NET PAY	421.11

TF TECHNOFILE CORPORATION

Check No. 2689412

Date Issued 05/11/09

Pay to FAISAL HADDAD

FOUR HUNDRED TWENTY-ONE DOLLARS AND ELEVEN CENTS

***$421.11

Anna Rosario

23. Faisal's regular pay is ____.
Ⓐ $16.00 an hour
Ⓑ $24.00 an hour
Ⓒ $32.00 an hour
Ⓓ $35.00 an hour

24. He worked a total of ____ during this pay period.
Ⓐ 16 hours
Ⓑ 24 hours
Ⓒ 35 hours
Ⓓ 38 hours

25. A pay period at the Technofile Corporation is ____.
Ⓐ a day
Ⓑ a week
Ⓒ a month
Ⓓ a year

26. Faisal earned ____ during this pay period before taxes and other deductions.
Ⓐ $72.00
Ⓑ $560.00
Ⓒ $632.00
Ⓓ $10,184.00

27. The deduction for state taxes since the beginning of the year is ____.
Ⓐ $31.60
Ⓑ $94.80
Ⓒ $170.64
Ⓓ $509.20

28. The company deducted a total of ____ from Faisal's salary during this pay period.
Ⓐ $40.25
Ⓑ $170.64
Ⓒ $210.89
Ⓓ $421.11

23 Ⓐ Ⓑ Ⓒ Ⓓ   25 Ⓐ Ⓑ Ⓒ Ⓓ   27 Ⓐ Ⓑ Ⓒ Ⓓ
24 Ⓐ Ⓑ Ⓒ Ⓓ   26 Ⓐ Ⓑ Ⓒ Ⓓ   28 Ⓐ Ⓑ Ⓒ Ⓓ

Go to the next page

E CLOZE READING: Small Talk at Work

Choose the correct answers to complete the paragraph.

"Small talk" at work is important. The short conversations that people have with

its their our co-workers show that they be was are 29 friendly. There are many
(A) (●) (C)   (A) (B) (C)

good questions to begin small talk: "What do did will 30 you do last weekend?" "What
                                           (A) (B) (C)

are you will going going to 31 do next weekend?" "Did you see the football game on TV
         (A)   (B)   (C)

yesterday tomorrow next week 32?" Other safe topics are hobbies, movies, TV programs,
(A)   (B)   (C)

and the weather weathers whether 33. You can talk about the news, but avoid
         (A)   (B)   (C)

to talk talking don't talk 34 about politics. Sharing Share You Share 35 information
(A)   (B)   (C)   (A)   (B)   (C)

about your family can be a good topic for small talk, but co-workers won't like

hear listen hearing 36 about serious family problems. Listening is also an important part
(A)   (B)   (C)

of small talk. Listening Listen You listen 37 carefully to what your co-workers are saying, and
                (A)   (B)   (C)

ask questions to show you're interested.

F LISTENING ASSESSMENT: Two Co-Workers Talking at the Office

Read and listen to the questions. Then listen to the conversation and answer the questions.

38. Who just had a baby?
    (A) Tonya.
    (B) Leona.
    (C) Ken's wife.
    (D) Ken's sister.

39. What are Tonya and Barry thinking about doing?
    (A) Buying a house.
    (B) Getting an apartment outside the city.
    (C) Moving to a new apartment in their building.
    (D) Buying a new TV.

40. How did Ken go to Tampa?
    (A) He went by bus.
    (B) He probably went by airplane.
    (C) He went by car.
    (D) This information isn't in the conversation.

29 (A) (B) (C) (D)   33 (A) (B) (C) (D)   37 (A) (B) (C) (D)
30 (A) (B) (C) (D)   34 (A) (B) (C) (D)   38 (A) (B) (C) (D)
31 (A) (B) (C) (D)   35 (A) (B) (C) (D)   39 (A) (B) (C) (D)
32 (A) (B) (C) (D)   36 (A) (B) (C) (D)   40 (A) (B) (C) (D)

Complete the form with your own information or make up any information you wish.

Form W-4

Purpose. Complete Form W-4 so that your employer can withhold the correct federal income tax from your pay.

Head of household. You are the head of household if you pay more than 50% of the costs of keeping up a home for yourself and your dependents.

Personal Allowances Worksheet

A	Enter "1" for **yourself** if no one else can claim you as a dependent.............................	**A** _____
B	Enter "1" if { • You are single and have only one job; or • You are married, have only one job, and your spouse does not work; or • Your wages from a second job or your spouse's wages are $1,500 or less. }	**B** _____
C	Enter "1" for your **spouse**. ---	**C** _____
D	Enter number of **dependents**.---	**D** _____
E	Enter "1" if you will file as **head of household** on your tax return.-------------------	**E** _____
F	Enter "1" if you have at least $1,500 of **child or dependent care expenses**.-----------	**F** _____
G	**Child Tax Credit** • If your total income is less than $58,000 ($86,000 if married), enter "2" for each child. • If your total income is between $58,000 and $84,000 ($86,000 and $119,000 if married), enter "1" for each child. --	**G** _____
H	Add lines A through G and enter total here.------------------------------------▶	**H** _____

Stop here and enter the number from line H on line 5 of Form W-4 below.

- -

Form **W-4**   **Employee's Withholding Allowance Certificate**

1 Type or print your first name and middle initial.	Last name	**2** Your social security number
Home address (number and street or rural route)	**3** ☐ Single ☐ Married ☐ Married, but withhold at higher Single rate.	
City or town, state, and ZIP code	**4** If your last name is different from the one on your social security card, check here. You must call 1-800-772-1213 for a replacement card. ☐	

5 Total number of allowances you are claiming (from line **H** above)-------------------	**5**	
6 Additional amount, if any, you want withheld from each paycheck ---------------------	**6**	
7 I claim exemption from withholding, and I meet **both** of the following conditions. • Last year I had a right to a refund of **all** federal income tax withheld because I had **no** tax liability **and** • This year I expect a refund of **all** federal income tax withheld because I expect to have **no** tax liability. If you meet both conditions write "Exempt" here ----------------------------▶	**7**	

Under penalties of perjury, I declare that I have examined this certificate and to the best of my knowledge and belief, it is true, correct, and complete.

Employee's signature
(Form is not valid
unless you sign it.) ▶   **Date** ▶

I can ask and answer these questions:

Ask Answer

☐ ☐ What did you do last weekend?
☐ ☐ What are you going to do next weekend?

Ask Answer

☐ ☐ What do you enjoy doing in your free time?
☐ ☐ What do you avoid doing whenever you can?

STOP

A   HEALTH & NUTRITION

Example:

I'd like to make _____.
- Ⓐ cancel
- Ⓑ reschedule
- ⬤ an appointment
- Ⓓ a doctor's office

1. Can you _____ on Friday at 10:00?
- Ⓐ convenient
- Ⓑ convenient time
- Ⓒ come in
- Ⓓ would be fine

2. You should have a physical _____ every year.
- Ⓐ history
- Ⓑ examination
- Ⓒ vaccination
- Ⓓ prescription

3. I have to get a _____ shot.
- Ⓐ dental
- Ⓑ clinic
- Ⓒ cholesterol
- Ⓓ flu

4. Do you take any prescription _____?
- Ⓐ drugs
- Ⓑ operations
- Ⓒ tests
- Ⓓ diseases

5. The _____ on the food pyramid show the different food groups.
- Ⓐ grains
- Ⓑ products
- Ⓒ steps
- Ⓓ stripes

6. Dark green and orange vegetables contain more _____ than starchy vegetables.
- Ⓐ juice
- Ⓑ dairy products
- Ⓒ nutrients
- Ⓓ cholesterol

7. The oil from _____ is good for your heart.
- Ⓐ fish
- Ⓑ butter
- Ⓒ margarine
- Ⓓ ice cream

8. The grain group consists of foods made from wheat, rice, or _____.
- Ⓐ vegetables
- Ⓑ oils
- Ⓒ corn
- Ⓓ milk

9. I have a bad cough. I'm going to _____.
- Ⓐ go to the emergency room
- Ⓑ go to the clinic
- Ⓒ call 911
- Ⓓ get a vaccination

1 Ⓐ Ⓑ Ⓒ Ⓓ   4 Ⓐ Ⓑ Ⓒ Ⓓ   7 Ⓐ Ⓑ Ⓒ Ⓓ
2 Ⓐ Ⓑ Ⓒ Ⓓ   5 Ⓐ Ⓑ Ⓒ Ⓓ   8 Ⓐ Ⓑ Ⓒ Ⓓ
3 Ⓐ Ⓑ Ⓒ Ⓓ   6 Ⓐ Ⓑ Ⓒ Ⓓ   9 Ⓐ Ⓑ Ⓒ Ⓓ

B GRAMMAR IN CONTEXT: Common Medical & Dental Problems

Example:
How long _____ coughing like this?
- Ⓐ are you
- Ⓑ you are
- Ⓒ you've been
- ⬤ have you been

10. _____ a few days.
- Ⓐ Since
- Ⓑ From
- Ⓒ With
- Ⓓ For

11. How long have your legs _____ swollen?
- Ⓐ are
- Ⓑ being
- Ⓒ been
- Ⓓ be

12. _____ last Monday.
- Ⓐ Since
- Ⓑ During
- Ⓒ For
- Ⓓ Began

13. When _____ first see these bruises on your arm?
- Ⓐ you did
- Ⓑ did you
- Ⓒ you have
- Ⓓ have you

14. I don't know. _____ them for a while.
- Ⓐ I'll have
- Ⓑ I'm having
- Ⓒ I had
- Ⓓ I've had

15. _____ this area here feel tender?
- Ⓐ Do
- Ⓑ Does
- Ⓒ Have
- Ⓓ Has

16. Ouch! Yes. _____ felt tender since I fell down the stairs.
- Ⓐ I
- Ⓑ They have
- Ⓒ It has
- Ⓓ I was

17. You have a _____. I can take care of it today.
- Ⓐ filling
- Ⓑ tooth
- Ⓒ gum
- Ⓓ cavity

18. Can I have a silver _____?
- Ⓐ filling
- Ⓑ tooth
- Ⓒ gum
- Ⓓ cavity

Yes, you can.

Okay.

10 Ⓐ Ⓑ Ⓒ Ⓓ   13 Ⓐ Ⓑ Ⓒ Ⓓ   15 Ⓐ Ⓑ Ⓒ Ⓓ   17 Ⓐ Ⓑ Ⓒ Ⓓ

11 Ⓐ Ⓑ Ⓒ Ⓓ   14 Ⓐ Ⓑ Ⓒ Ⓓ   16 Ⓐ Ⓑ Ⓒ Ⓓ   18 Ⓐ Ⓑ Ⓒ Ⓓ

12 Ⓐ Ⓑ Ⓒ Ⓓ

Go to the next page ⟩

C **READING: Medical Appointment Cards**

These people have medical appointments during the next few months. Read the appointment cards. Then do Numbers 19 through 22.

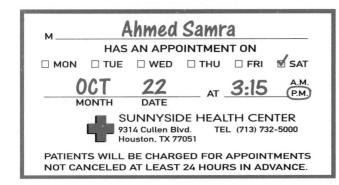

COMMUNITY MEDICAL CLINIC
4600 N. Federal Highway, Miami, FL 33137

Quan Vu

HAS AN APPOINTMENT ON

Mon.	Oct.	10th	at	11	(A.M.) P.M.
DAY	MONTH	DATE			

IF UNABLE TO KEEP THIS APPOINTMENT, PLEASE GIVE ONE DAY ADVANCE NOTICE.
TELEPHONE: (305) 576-7000

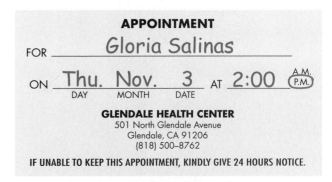

APPOINTMENT

FOR _Gloria Salinas_

ON _Thu._ _Nov._ _3_ AT _2:00_ (P.M.)
    DAY   MONTH   DATE

GLENDALE HEALTH CENTER
501 North Glendale Avenue
Glendale, CA 91206
(818) 500-8762

IF UNABLE TO KEEP THIS APPOINTMENT, KINDLY GIVE 24 HOURS NOTICE.

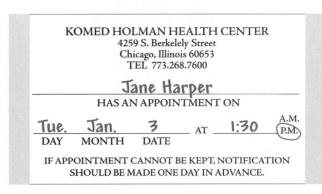

M _Ahmed Samra_

HAS AN APPOINTMENT ON

☐ MON ☐ TUE ☐ WED ☐ THU ☐ FRI ☑ SAT

OCT	22	AT	3:15	A.M. (P.M.)
MONTH	DATE			

✚ **SUNNYSIDE HEALTH CENTER**
9314 Cullen Blvd. TEL (713) 732-5000
Houston, TX 77051

**PATIENTS WILL BE CHARGED FOR APPOINTMENTS
NOT CANCELED AT LEAST 24 HOURS IN ADVANCE.**

KOMED HOLMAN HEALTH CENTER
4259 S. Berkelely Street
Chicago, Illinois 60653
TEL 773.268.7600

Jane Harper

HAS AN APPOINTMENT ON

Tue.	Jan.	3	AT	1:30	A.M. (P.M.)
DAY	MONTH	DATE			

IF APPOINTMENT CANNOT BE KEPT, NOTIFICATION
SHOULD BE MADE ONE DAY IN ADVANCE.

---

19. Which day of the week is Gloria's appointment?
    Ⓐ Tuesday
    Ⓑ Thursday
    Ⓒ November
    Ⓓ the 3rd

20. Which patient has an appointment in the morning?
    Ⓐ Jane Harper
    Ⓑ Gloria Salinas
    Ⓒ Ahmed Samra
    Ⓓ Quan Vu

21. Which health center is definitely open during part of the weekend?
    Ⓐ Community Medical Clinic
    Ⓑ Glendale Health Center
    Ⓒ Sunnyside Health Center
    Ⓓ Komed Holman Health Center

22. Whose appointment is next year?
    Ⓐ Jane Harper
    Ⓑ Gloria Salinas
    Ⓒ Ahmed Samra
    Ⓓ Quan Vu

....

19 Ⓐ Ⓑ Ⓒ Ⓓ   20 Ⓐ Ⓑ Ⓒ Ⓓ   21 Ⓐ Ⓑ Ⓒ Ⓓ   22 Ⓐ Ⓑ Ⓒ Ⓓ

Look at the illustrations. Choose the correct answer.

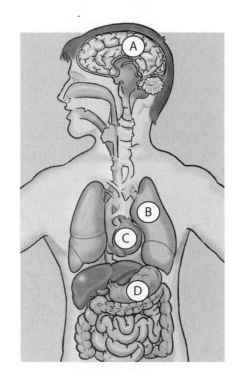

Example: stomach   Ⓐ Ⓑ Ⓒ ●

23. brain   Ⓐ Ⓑ Ⓒ Ⓓ

24. heart   Ⓐ Ⓑ Ⓒ Ⓓ

25. lungs   Ⓐ Ⓑ Ⓒ Ⓓ

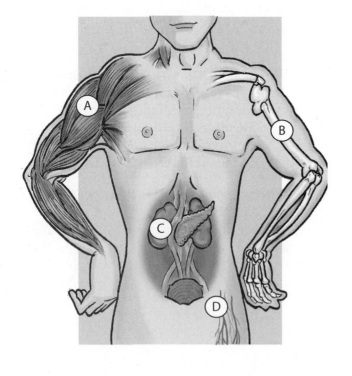

26. veins   Ⓐ Ⓑ Ⓒ Ⓓ

27. bones   Ⓐ Ⓑ Ⓒ Ⓓ

28. kidneys   Ⓐ Ⓑ Ⓒ Ⓓ

29. muscles   Ⓐ Ⓑ Ⓒ Ⓓ

E CLOZE READING: Public Health Information

Choose the correct answers to complete the newspaper article.

New Health Center Opens

WARNER—The new Downtown Health Center opened yesterday. The

examination	clinic	emergency
(A)	●	(C)

offers health care to all city residents. It is a drop-in medical center,

so no

service	routine	appointment
(A)	(B)	(C)

30 is necessary. For patients who don't understand English well,

vaccination	translation	medication
(A)	(B)	(C)

31 is available in 15 different languages. Patients pay for medical

care based on how much they earn since the clinic's fees are on a sliding

scale	range	care
(A)	(B)	(C)

32. Patients

can have a physical

guideline	operation	examination
(A)	(B)	(C)

33 every year, including a

cholesterol	tetanus	skin
(A)	(B)	(C)

34 blood test and other screening tests. The clinic also provides flu shots and

other

prescriptions	vaccinations	schedules
(A)	(B)	(C)

35. It is across the street from Warner General Hospital,

a full-service hospital with 500 beds and a 24-hour

serious	911	emergency
(A)	(B)	(C)

36 room. Patients should

go there or call an ambulance for health problems such as

a cough	a broken leg	an earache
(A)	(B)	(C)

37.

Patients with routine medical problems should use the clinic.

F LISTENING ASSESSMENT: Calling about a Medical Appointment

Read and listen to the questions. Then listen to the conversation and answer the questions.

38. Why is Victoria calling the doctor's office?
- (A) To make a new appointment.
- (B) To cancel an appointment.
- (C) To reschedule an appointment.
- (D) To confirm an appointment.

39. When was she scheduled to come in?
- (A) Thu. Apr. 15 4:00
- (B) Tue. Apr. 20 11:00
- (C) Thu. Apr. 20 11:00
- (D) Tue. Apr. 13 10:00

40. When is her new appointment?
- (A) Thu. Apr. 15 4:00
- (B) Tue. Apr. 20 11:00
- (C) Thu. Apr. 20 11:00
- (D) Tue. Apr. 13 10:00

....

30 (A) (B) (C) (D)   33 (A) (B) (C) (D)   36 (A) (B) (C) (D)   39 (A) (B) (C) (D)

31 (A) (B) (C) (D)   34 (A) (B) (C) (D)   37 (A) (B) (C) (D)   40 (A) (B) (C) (D)

32 (A) (B) (C) (D)   35 (A) (B) (C) (D)   38 (A) (B) (C) (D)

Go to the next page ⟹

Complete the form with your own information or make up any information you wish.

MEDICAL HISTORY

Name _____ Date of Birth _____

List the medications you are now taking. Include non-prescription drugs and vitamins.

_____

List any allergies you have to drugs, food, or other items. _____

_____

List any operations you have had, including the year. _____

_____

Please check if you have had any of the following health problems.

_____ chicken pox	_____ diabetes	_____ depression
_____ measles	_____ tuberculosis	_____ frequent earaches
_____ mumps	_____ cancer	_____ severe headaches
_____ asthma	_____ AIDS	_____ back problems
_____ heart disease	_____ kidney disease	_____ frequent colds
_____ high blood pressure	_____ liver disease (hepatitis)	_____ stomach problems
_____ pneumonia	_____ influenza	_____ loss of appetite

FAMILY HISTORY

Please check if anyone in your family (parents, siblings, grandparents, children) has had any of the following illnesses.

_____ asthma	_____ diabetes	_____ AIDS
_____ heart disease	_____ tuberculosis	_____ kidney disease
_____ high blood pressure	_____ cancer	_____ liver disease

RECORD OF IMMUNIZATIONS

Please check if you had any of the following vaccinations or tests, and fill in the year of the most recent ones.

	Year
_____ measles	
_____ mumps	
_____ chicken pox	
_____ tetanus	

	Year
_____ tuberculosis test	
_____ hepatitis B	
_____ influenza	
_____ pneumonia	

H SPEAKING ASSESSMENT

I can ask and answer these questions:

Ask Answer
☐ ☐ How often do you have a physical examination at a doctor's office or a clinic?
☐ ☐ Where do you go for medical care?

Ask Answer
☐ ☐ What vegetables and fruit do you eat?
☐ ☐ What foods should you eat more of?
☐ ☐ What foods should you eat less of?

STOP

A SHOPPING

Example:

I'm _____ a pair of pants.
- Ⓐ want
- Ⓑ need
- Ⓒ looking
- ⬤ looking for

1. This dress is 20% off this week. We're having a special _____.
   - Ⓐ regular price
   - Ⓑ half-price
   - Ⓒ sale
   - Ⓓ reduced

2. You can try on these pants in the _____.
   - Ⓐ mall
   - Ⓑ cleaner's
   - Ⓒ pants room
   - Ⓓ dressing room

3. I like to buy things when they're _____.
   - Ⓐ discount
   - Ⓑ on sale
   - Ⓒ the sign on the rack
   - Ⓓ bargain

4. My jacket size is _____.
   - Ⓐ 20% off
   - Ⓑ half-price
   - Ⓒ large
   - Ⓓ reduced

5. I don't want to exchange it. I'd like _____, please.
   - Ⓐ the matter
   - Ⓑ a return
   - Ⓒ a receipt
   - Ⓓ a refund

6. All our shirts are 15 _____ off the regular price this week.
   - Ⓐ percent
   - Ⓑ price
   - Ⓒ reduced
   - Ⓓ half

7. You can use this coupon until the _____.
   - Ⓐ regular price
   - Ⓑ expiration date
   - Ⓒ newspaper ad
   - Ⓓ refund

8. These tee shirts are usually $16, but they're only $12 this week. They're _____.
   - Ⓐ 10% off
   - Ⓑ 20% off
   - Ⓒ 25% off
   - Ⓓ half-price

9. All our $60 men's jeans are $40 this week. They're _____ the regular price.
   - Ⓐ 1/3 off
   - Ⓑ 1/2 off
   - Ⓒ 20% off
   - Ⓓ 40% off

....

1 Ⓐ Ⓑ Ⓒ Ⓓ   4 Ⓐ Ⓑ Ⓒ Ⓓ   7 Ⓐ Ⓑ Ⓒ Ⓓ

2 Ⓐ Ⓑ Ⓒ Ⓓ   5 Ⓐ Ⓑ Ⓒ Ⓓ   8 Ⓐ Ⓑ Ⓒ Ⓓ

3 Ⓐ Ⓑ Ⓒ Ⓓ   6 Ⓐ Ⓑ Ⓒ Ⓓ   9 Ⓐ Ⓑ Ⓒ Ⓓ

Go to the next page ⟩

Example:

I'd like to exchange _____ jacket.
- ● A this
- Ⓑ that
- Ⓒ these
- Ⓓ those

RETURN POLICY

10. What's the matter with _____?
- Ⓐ you
- Ⓑ that
- Ⓒ this
- Ⓓ it

11. Three buttons _____ missing.
- Ⓐ be
- Ⓑ is
- Ⓒ are
- Ⓓ will be

12. All right. Please get another jacket from the rack, _____ here, and I'll be happy to help you.
- Ⓐ bring back
- Ⓑ bring it back
- Ⓒ bring back it
- Ⓓ it bring back

13. I'd like to return _____ pants.
- Ⓐ this
- Ⓑ that
- Ⓒ these
- Ⓓ those

14. What's the matter with _____?
- Ⓐ it
- Ⓑ you
- Ⓒ those
- Ⓓ them

15. The zipper _____ broken.
- Ⓐ be
- Ⓑ is
- Ⓒ are
- Ⓓ did

16. _____ your receipt?
- Ⓐ You have
- Ⓑ Do have
- Ⓒ Do you have
- Ⓓ You do have

17. Yes. _____
- Ⓐ Here it is.
- Ⓑ Here I am.
- Ⓒ Here they are.
- Ⓓ It is.

18. _____ exchange them?
- Ⓐ Do you like to
- Ⓑ You do like to
- Ⓒ You would like to
- Ⓓ Would you like to

19. No, thank you. _____ a refund, please.
- Ⓐ I like
- Ⓑ I'd like
- Ⓒ I'll like
- Ⓓ You give

20. Okay. Here's our merchandise return form. Please _____ and I'll give you a refund.
- Ⓐ fill
- Ⓑ fill out
- Ⓒ fill out it
- Ⓓ fill it out

· ·

10 Ⓐ Ⓑ Ⓒ Ⓓ   13 Ⓐ Ⓑ Ⓒ Ⓓ   16 Ⓐ Ⓑ Ⓒ Ⓓ   19 Ⓐ Ⓑ Ⓒ Ⓓ

11 Ⓐ Ⓑ Ⓒ Ⓓ   14 Ⓐ Ⓑ Ⓒ Ⓓ   17 Ⓐ Ⓑ Ⓒ Ⓓ   20 Ⓐ Ⓑ Ⓒ Ⓓ

12 Ⓐ Ⓑ Ⓒ Ⓓ   15 Ⓐ Ⓑ Ⓒ Ⓓ   18 Ⓐ Ⓑ Ⓒ Ⓓ

Go to the next page ▷

Name _____   Date _____

C READING: A Store Advertisement

Look at the clothing store advertisement. Then do Numbers 21 through 24.

CARTER'S DEPARTMENT STORE

Biggest Sale of the Year!!!
Thursday thru Saturday, October 10-12

$19.99
50%–60% off
Men's dress shirts
Orig. $40-$50

Lana Lee tee shirts
Orig. $20
NOW 2/$25 OR $15 EACH

Speedway Running Shoes
Reg. $80
SALE $40

Warner Men's Jeans
Reg. $40
SALE $30

All Nina Sanders skirts
HALF PRICE
SALE $25

---

21. During the sale, Speedway Running Shoes are _____.
   Ⓐ 10% off
   Ⓑ 40% off
   Ⓒ $80.00
   Ⓓ half-price

22. Fatima is going to buy four tee shirts during the sale. How much is she going to spend?
   Ⓐ $50
   Ⓑ $60
   Ⓒ $70
   Ⓓ $80

23. The regular price of Nina Sanders skirts is _____.
   Ⓐ $25
   Ⓑ $50
   Ⓒ $75
   Ⓓ $100

24. The men's jeans are _____ during the sale.
   Ⓐ 10% off
   Ⓑ 20% off
   Ⓒ 25% off
   Ⓓ 30% off

---

21 Ⓐ Ⓑ Ⓒ Ⓓ   22 Ⓐ Ⓑ Ⓒ Ⓓ   23 Ⓐ Ⓑ Ⓒ Ⓓ   24 Ⓐ Ⓑ Ⓒ Ⓓ

Go to the next page ⟹   T45

Look at the coupons for these food products. Then do Numbers 25 through 30.

25. You bought a loaf of Alan's bread with a coupon and paid $2.00. The original price was _____.
   Ⓐ $1.50
   Ⓑ $2.00
   Ⓒ $2.50
   Ⓓ $3.00

26. A box of Happy Heart cereal costs $3.00. With a coupon you pay _____ for three boxes.
   Ⓐ $5.00
   Ⓑ $6.00
   Ⓒ $7.50
   Ⓓ $9.00

27. You can't use the coupon for _____ after September 18, 2012.
   Ⓐ Bob & Joe's Ice Cream
   Ⓑ Maxima Coffee
   Ⓒ Farmtown Yogurt
   Ⓓ Pollyana Jam

28. Ramona bought one pint of Bob & Joe's Ice Cream. The regular price is $4.50. She paid _____.
   Ⓐ $1.00
   Ⓑ $3.50
   Ⓒ $4.00
   Ⓓ $4.50

29. A 6 oz. container of Farmtown Yogurt costs $1.00. With a coupon you pay a total of _____ when you buy ten.
   Ⓐ $9.00
   Ⓑ $9.50
   Ⓒ $10.00
   Ⓓ 90¢

30. You bought two cans of Maxima Coffee with a coupon and paid $9.00. The regular price of one can is _____.
   Ⓐ $4.50
   Ⓑ $5.00
   Ⓒ $5.50
   Ⓓ $6.00

25 Ⓐ Ⓑ Ⓒ Ⓓ   27 Ⓐ Ⓑ Ⓒ Ⓓ   29 Ⓐ Ⓑ Ⓒ Ⓓ

26 Ⓐ Ⓑ Ⓒ Ⓓ   28 Ⓐ Ⓑ Ⓒ Ⓓ   30 Ⓐ Ⓑ Ⓒ Ⓓ

Go to the next page

Name _____   Date _____

E CLOZE READING: A Store Return Policy

Choose the correct answers to complete the sign in a store's Customer Service Department.

Pratt's Department Store
Our Return Policy

- You may   receipt(A)   refund(B)   return(●)   most items within 90 days of the date of purchase.

- We will   back(A)   take back(B)   take them back(C) ³¹ computers and printers only within 45 days

  of the date of purchase.

- If you want to return CDs or DVDs, you must   bring(A)   bring back(B)   bring them back(C) ³²

  within 30 days of the date of purchase, and they must be   opened(A)   unopened(B)   on sale(C) ³³.

- We cannot accept returns on items marked Final   Sale(A)   Refund(B)   Credit(C) ³⁴.

- To receive a refund, you must provide your   return(A)   receipt(B)   purchase(C) ³⁵ for the item. If

  you don't have it, you can   buy(A)   accept(B)   exchange(C) ³⁶ the item for another one or you can

  receive a gift card with a store credit for the amount of the purchase.

- You may return a defective item at any time, and we will   repair(A)   break(B)   buy(C) ³⁷ it or give

  you a new item.

F LISTENING ASSESSMENT: Returning Items to a Store

Read and listen to the questions. Then listen to the conversation and answer the questions.

38. How many items is the customer returning to the store?
- (A) One.
- (B) Two.
- (C) Three.
- (D) Four.

39. What's the matter with the blouse?
- (A) A button is missing.
- (B) Two buttons are missing.
- (C) A sleeve is stained.
- (D) The sleeves are stained.

40. Why can't the customer receive a refund?
- (A) The coat and the blouse are defective.
- (B) The customer wants to exchange the items.
- (C) The customer doesn't have a gift card.
- (D) The customer doesn't have the receipt.

G WRITING ASSESSMENT: A Product Return Form

You are returning an item to a store in your community. Complete the form with your personal information, and make up information about the product you are returning.

PRODUCT RETURN FORM

1. CUSTOMER INFORMATION

Name _____

Address _____

City _____ State _____ Zip Code _____

Telephone: Home (_____) _____-_____   Work (_____) _____-_____

2. PRODUCT INFORMATION

Product being returned: _____

Store where purchased (name, city, state): _____

Purchase date: _____

Please describe problem with product: _____

_____

3. REFUND/EXCHANGE INFORMATION

Please check one:

_____ I request a refund. (Store receipt required.)

_____ I will exchange the product for another one of the same item.

_____ I request a store credit for the amount of the purchase.

_____ Other (Explain: _____)

Customer Signature: _____ Today's Date: _____

H SPEAKING ASSESSMENT

I can ask and answer these questions:

Ask	Answer		Ask	Answer		Ask	Answer	
☐	☐	Where do you shop for clothing?	☐	☐	Have you ever bought something on sale?	☐	☐	Have you ever returned an item to a store?
☐	☐	What kind of clothing do you like to wear?	☐	☐	What did you buy, and where?	☐	☐	What did you return, and where?

STOP

A WORKPLACE COMMUNICATION & CAREER ADVANCEMENT

Example:

Excuse me. Can you _____?
- Ⓐ I help
- Ⓑ my help
- ⬤ help me
- Ⓓ me help

1. Please _____ make a copy.
   - Ⓐ how to
   - Ⓑ show me how
   - Ⓒ you show me how to
   - Ⓓ show me how to

2. _____, add the water. Then, press the ON button.
   - Ⓐ Sure
   - Ⓑ First
   - Ⓒ Finally
   - Ⓓ And finally

3. I'm friendly at work. I _____ my co-workers.
   - Ⓐ get
   - Ⓑ get along
   - Ⓒ get along with
   - Ⓓ along with

4. I try to always have a positive _____ at work.
   - Ⓐ compliment
   - Ⓑ attitude
   - Ⓒ feedback
   - Ⓓ promotion

5. Appropriate clothes and good grooming are important parts of your _____ at work.
   - Ⓐ appearance
   - Ⓑ opportunity
   - Ⓒ energy
   - Ⓓ creativity

6. When a co-worker does something well, _____.
   - Ⓐ apologize
   - Ⓑ complain
   - Ⓒ volunteer
   - Ⓓ give a compliment

7. It's important to continue your _____ to learn new skills.
   - Ⓐ promotion
   - Ⓑ evaluation
   - Ⓒ education
   - Ⓓ presentation

8. If you want to move ahead at work, ask for more _____.
   - Ⓐ skills
   - Ⓑ responsibilities
   - Ⓒ compliments
   - Ⓓ grades

9. I'm going to take a _____ course so that my memos, letters, and reports are better.
   - Ⓐ Customer Service
   - Ⓑ Bookkeeping
   - Ⓒ Public Speaking
   - Ⓓ Business Writing

1 Ⓐ Ⓑ Ⓒ Ⓓ   4 Ⓐ Ⓑ Ⓒ Ⓓ   7 Ⓐ Ⓑ Ⓒ Ⓓ
2 Ⓐ Ⓑ Ⓒ Ⓓ   5 Ⓐ Ⓑ Ⓒ Ⓓ   8 Ⓐ Ⓑ Ⓒ Ⓓ
3 Ⓐ Ⓑ Ⓒ Ⓓ   6 Ⓐ Ⓑ Ⓒ Ⓓ   9 Ⓐ Ⓑ Ⓒ Ⓓ

B GRAMMAR IN CONTEXT: Giving & Following a Sequence of Instructions

Example:

Excuse me, Rosa. _____ help me?
- Ⓐ I can
- Ⓑ You can
- Ⓒ Can I
- ⬤ Can you

10. Sure. _____ help?
- Ⓐ How I can
- Ⓑ How you can
- Ⓒ How can I
- Ⓓ How can you

11. _____ how to turn on the alarm system?
- Ⓐ You can show me
- Ⓑ Can you show me
- Ⓒ I can show you
- Ⓓ Can I show you

12. Sure. _____
- Ⓐ I'll be happy.
- Ⓑ I'll be happy to.
- Ⓒ You'll be happy.
- Ⓓ You'll be happy to.

13. _____
- Ⓐ I see.
- Ⓑ That's correct.
- Ⓒ You're welcome.
- Ⓓ Thanks.

14. _____, close the door. _____, enter the code.
- Ⓐ Then . . . After that
- Ⓑ Then . . . First
- Ⓒ First . . . Then
- Ⓓ Finally . . . Then

15. _____
- Ⓐ I see.
- Ⓑ You see.
- Ⓒ Yes. That's correct.
- Ⓓ Excuse me.

16. _____, press ON. _____, leave the building.
- Ⓐ First . . . Then
- Ⓑ First . . . And finally
- Ⓒ After that . . . First
- Ⓓ After that . . . And finally

17. I press ON and leave the building. _____
- Ⓐ Can you help me?
- Ⓑ How can I help?
- Ⓒ Is that right?
- Ⓓ Are you right?

18. Yes. _____
- Ⓐ I'm correct.
- Ⓑ That's correct.
- Ⓒ Thanks very much.
- Ⓓ That isn't right.

....

10 Ⓐ Ⓑ Ⓒ Ⓓ   13 Ⓐ Ⓑ Ⓒ Ⓓ   16 Ⓐ Ⓑ Ⓒ Ⓓ

11 Ⓐ Ⓑ Ⓒ Ⓓ   14 Ⓐ Ⓑ Ⓒ Ⓓ   17 Ⓐ Ⓑ Ⓒ Ⓓ

12 Ⓐ Ⓑ Ⓒ Ⓓ   15 Ⓐ Ⓑ Ⓒ Ⓓ   18 Ⓐ Ⓑ Ⓒ Ⓓ

Go to the next page ⟩

READING: A Job Performance Evaluation

Look at this employee's job performance evaluation. Then do Numbers 19 through 22.

Employee Name _Manuel Garcia_   Position _Stock clerk_

	Excellent	Good	Needs Improvement	Unsatisfactory
The employee understands the job responsibilities.	✓			
The employee has the skills needed to do the job.		✓		
The employee communicates clearly.			✓	
The employee listens carefully to supervisors and co-workers.			✓	
The employee gets along well with co-workers.		✓		
The employee has a positive attitude.	✓			
The employee is dependable and hardworking.	✓			
The employee is polite and friendly with customers.				
The employee solves problems creatively.			✓	
The employee dresses appropriately.		✓		
The employee is well groomed.	✓			
The employee learns from feedback.			✓	
The employee continues to learn new skills.	✓			

Employee's Signature _Manuel Garcia_   Date of Evaluation _12/14/09_

Evaluated by (Print) _Larissa Silver_   Evaluator's Signature _Larissa Silver_

19. The employee has _____ grades that are Excellent or Good.
   Ⓐ three
   Ⓑ five
   Ⓒ eight
   Ⓓ twelve

20. Larissa is Manuel Garcia's _____.
   Ⓐ supervisor
   Ⓑ stock clerk
   Ⓒ employee
   Ⓓ customer

21. We can infer that _____.
   Ⓐ the employee doesn't like his job
   Ⓑ the employee doesn't work hard
   Ⓒ the employee doesn't have very good listening and speaking skills
   Ⓓ the employee isn't dependable

22. One line of the evaluation form is not filled in. This is probably because _____.
   Ⓐ the employee isn't friendly with customers
   Ⓑ the employee isn't polite with customers
   Ⓒ customers complain about the employee
   Ⓓ the employee doesn't communicate with customers in his job

19 Ⓐ Ⓑ Ⓒ Ⓓ   20 Ⓐ Ⓑ Ⓒ Ⓓ   21 Ⓐ Ⓑ Ⓒ Ⓓ   22 Ⓐ Ⓑ Ⓒ Ⓓ

Look at the adult education catalog. Then do Numbers 23 through 26.

ADULT EDUCATION COURSES—FALL TERM

BUSINESS

BUS 101 Business Procedures—M, W, F
Learn the procedures in a business office. Topics include filing, telephone skills, receiving and sending mail, organizing meetings and conferences, scheduling appointments, making travel reservations, and time management.

BUS 105 Business Writing—M, W
This course helps students learn to write clear and concise business letters, memos, and reports.

BUS 201 Bookkeeping—M, Tu, W, Th, F
This course prepares students for the national Certified Bookkeeper examination. Topics include payroll (paying wages, reporting taxes) and inventory.

BUS 205 Entrepreneurship—W, F
Learn how to start and operate your own business. Each student will develop a business plan.

COMPUTERS

COM 101 Microsoft Word I—Tu, Th
Students will learn to create documents with the popular word processing software.

COM 102 Microsoft Outlook—F
Learn to use Microsoft Outlook to send, receive, and organize electronic mail.

COM 106 Excel Spreadsheets—Tu, Th
Balancing a checkbook and calculating family expenses is easier with Excel software. This course covers the basics of spreadsheets.

COM 201 Microsoft Word II—W, Th, F
Use the advanced features of Word to create documents with charts. Students will also learn to create newsletters and flyers.

COM 203 PowerPoint Presentations—M, F
Learn to create professional-looking presentations that include graphs, charts, and pictures using PowerPoint.

CULINARY ARTS

CA 100 Food Preparation—M, Tu, W, Th, F
Students learn kitchen procedures and basic recipes for an entry-level position as a Food and Beverage Specialist in a hotel, hospital, or restaurant kitchen.

CA 104 Food Sanitation—W, F
Learn how to prepare food safely. This course teaches health regulations and procedures and the reasons for them.

HEALTH SCIENCE

HS 101 CPR (Cardiopulmonary Resuscitation)—M
This course covers emergency procedures to follow when someone has stopped breathing or the heart has stopped beating. Red Cross certification.

---

23. Microsoft Word is software for _____.
    - Ⓐ giving presentations
    - Ⓑ sending and receiving e-mail
    - Ⓒ making spreadsheets
    - Ⓓ writing documents

24. Sonia and Mercedes are planning to start their own cleaning service company. They're going to take the course in _____ to prepare to open their business.
    - Ⓐ Entrepreneurship
    - Ⓑ Business Writing
    - Ⓒ CPR
    - Ⓓ Food Preparation

25. Julio can only take adult education courses on Tuesdays and Thursdays because of his work schedule. He's thinking about taking Course Number _____.
    - Ⓐ BUS 105
    - Ⓑ HS 101
    - Ⓒ COM 106
    - Ⓓ CA 100

26. Course Number _____ prepares students to take a national examination.
    - Ⓐ BUS 101
    - Ⓑ BUS 201
    - Ⓒ COM 106
    - Ⓓ CA 100

....

23 Ⓐ Ⓑ Ⓒ Ⓓ   24 Ⓐ Ⓑ Ⓒ Ⓓ   25 Ⓐ Ⓑ Ⓒ Ⓓ   26 Ⓐ Ⓑ Ⓒ Ⓓ

Go to the next page ⇨

E CLOZE READING: A Promotion at Work

Choose the correct answers to complete the memo.

CREATIVE COMPUTER SOLUTIONS

Interoffice Memorandum

TO: All Employees
FROM: Jane Hamilton, Director
SUBJECT: Promotion of Karima Mansoor

I am happy to announce the [evaluation (A) / **promotion** ● / education (C)] of Karima Mansoor to

the position of office manager. You all know that Karima has been doing an excellent job

as assistant manager. She's [hard work (A) / work hard (B) / hardworking (C)] ²⁷ and enthusiastic. She

[gets along (A) / knows (B) / takes care (C)] ²⁸ well with everyone in the office, she

[works (A) / communicates (B) / understands (C)] ²⁹ clearly, and she thinks [around (A) / inside (B) / outside (C)] ³⁰ the box

to find new ways to solve problems. Karima has recently finished a [grooming (A) / training (B) / solving (C)] ³¹

program that has prepared her well for this new position. She has completed a year of coursework in

[culinary (A) / sanitation (B) / business (C)] ³² procedures, and she has received the highest

[grades (A) / reports (B) / notes (C)] ³³ possible in this program. Karima's supervisor, Lidiya Sorreno, has given

Karima excellent job [appearance (A) / performance (B) / opportunity (C)] ³⁴ evaluations during the past three

years. Now that Lidiya has been promoted to the [position (A) / attitude (B) / evaluation (C)] ³⁵ of Director of

Personnel, we have decided that Karima is the best person to take Lidiya's place. We know that Karima

will do well with her new [supervisors (A) / responsibilities (B) / problems (C)] ³⁶. She has worked hard for our

company, and I know you agree that she [receives (A) / serves (B) / deserves (C)] ³⁷ this promotion.

---

27 Ⓐ Ⓑ Ⓒ Ⓓ	30 Ⓐ Ⓑ Ⓒ Ⓓ	33 Ⓐ Ⓑ Ⓒ Ⓓ	36 Ⓐ Ⓑ Ⓒ Ⓓ
28 Ⓐ Ⓑ Ⓒ Ⓓ	31 Ⓐ Ⓑ Ⓒ Ⓓ	34 Ⓐ Ⓑ Ⓒ Ⓓ	37 Ⓐ Ⓑ Ⓒ Ⓓ
29 Ⓐ Ⓑ Ⓒ Ⓓ	32 Ⓐ Ⓑ Ⓒ Ⓓ	35 Ⓐ Ⓑ Ⓒ Ⓓ	

Go to the next page → **T53**

Read and listen to the questions. Then listen to the conversation and answer the questions.

38. When is the copy machine ready to print?
- Ⓐ When the paper is regular size.
- Ⓑ When the Start button is green.
- Ⓒ When the lid is up.
- Ⓓ When the green light is on.

39. What does the employee need to copy?
- Ⓐ One regular-size page.
- Ⓑ One large-size page.
- Ⓒ Fifty regular-size pages.
- Ⓓ Fifty large-size pages.

40. How can someone copy a large map on this machine?
- Ⓐ Put it face down in the automatic document feeder.
- Ⓑ Put it face up in the automatic document feeder.
- Ⓒ Put it face down on the glass.
- Ⓓ Put it face up on the glass.

G WRITING ASSESSMENT: Your Education History & Education Plan

Fill out the form. Write information about the schools you have attended, the skills you have, and your education plans for the future.

EDUCATION HISTORY

Dates _____   Degree or certificate _____

School, City, State _____

Dates _____   Degree or certificate _____

School, City, State _____

Dates _____   Degree or certificate _____

School, City, State _____

SKILLS
_____

EDUCATION PLANS FOR THE FUTURE

What you plan to study:	Where (Name or type of school):	When (Year):
_____	_____	_____
_____	_____	_____
_____	_____	_____

H SPEAKING ASSESSMENT

I can ask and answer these questions:

Ask Answer
- ☐ ☐ Tell me about your skills.
- ☐ ☐ Tell me about your educational background.

Ask Answer
- ☐ ☐ What job do you want in the future?
- ☐ ☐ What new skills do you want to learn in the future?

STOP

APPENDIX

Listening Scripts

Page 7 Exercise H

Listen to each question and then complete the answer.

1. Does Jim like to play soccer?
2. Is Alice working today?
3. Are those students staying after school today?
4. Do Mr. and Mrs. Jackson work hard?
5. Does your wife still write poetry?
6. Is it raining?
7. Is he busy?
8. Do you have to leave?
9. Does your sister play the violin?
10. Is your brother studying in the library?
11. Are you wearing a necklace today?
12. Do you and your husband go camping very often?
13. Is your niece doing her homework?
14. Are they still chatting online?
15. Do you and your friends play Scrabble very often?

Page 13 Exercise B

Listen and circle the correct answer.

1. They work.
2. They worked.
3. We study English.
4. I waited for the bus.
5. We visit our friends.
6. She met important people.
7. He taught Chinese.
8. She delivers the mail.
9. I wrote letters to my friends.
10. I ride my bicycle to work.
11. He sleeps very well.
12. I had a terrible headache.

Page 26 Exercise C

Listen and choose the time of the action.

1. My daughter is going to sing Broadway show tunes in her high school show.
2. Janet bought a new dress for her friend's party.
3. Are you going to go out with George?
4. I went shopping at the new mall.
5. How did you poke yourself in the eye?
6. Who's going to prepare dinner?
7. Did the baby sleep well?
8. I'm really looking forward to Saturday night.
9. Is your son going to play games on his computer?
10. We're going to complain to the landlord about the heat in our apartment.
11. We bought a dozen donuts.
12. I'm going to take astronomy.

Page 33 Exercise L

Listen to each story. Then answer the questions.

What Are Mr. and Mrs. Miller Looking Forward to?

Mr. and Mrs. Miller moved into their new house in Los Angeles last week. They're happy because the house has a large, bright living room and a big, beautiful yard. They're looking forward to life in their new home. Every weekend they'll be able to relax in their living room and enjoy the beautiful California weather in their big, beautiful yard. But this weekend Mr. and Mrs. Miller won't be relaxing. They're going to be very busy. First, they're going to repaint the living room. Then, they're going to assemble their new computer and VCR. And finally, they're going to plant some flowers in their yard. They'll finally be able to relax NEXT weekend.

What's Jonathan Looking Forward to?

I'm so excited! I'm sitting at my computer in my office, but I'm not thinking about my work today. I'm thinking about next weekend because next Saturday is the day I'll be getting married. After the wedding, my wife and I will be going to Hawaii for a week. I can't wait! For one week, we won't be working, we won't be cooking, we won't be cleaning, and we won't be paying bills. We'll be swimming in the ocean, relaxing on the beach, and eating in fantastic restaurants.

What's Mrs. Grant Looking Forward to?

Mrs. Grant is going to retire this year, and she's really looking forward to her new life. She won't be getting up early every morning and taking the bus to work. She'll be able to sleep late every day of the week. She'll read books, she'll work in her garden, and she'll go to museums with her friends. And she's very happy that she'll be able to spend more time with her grandchildren. She'll take them to the park to feed the birds, she'll take them to the zoo to see the animals, and she'll baby-sit when her son and daughter-in-law go out on Saturday nights.

Page 35 Exercise E

Listen to each question and then complete the answer.

Ex. Does your brother like to swim?
1. Are you going to buy donuts tomorrow?
2. Will Jennifer and John see each other again soon?
3. Doctor, did I sprain my ankle?
4. Does Tommy have a black eye?
5. Is your daughter practicing the violin?
6. Do you and your husband go to the movies very often?

7. Does Diane go out with her boyfriend every Saturday evening?
8. Will you and your wife be visiting us tonight?

Page 36 Exercise B

Listen and choose the word you hear.

1. I've ridden them for many years.
2. Yes. I've taken French.
3. I'm giving injections.
4. I've driven one for many years.
5. Yes. I've written it.
6. I'm drawing it right now.
7. I've spoken it for many years.
8. Yes. I've drawn that.

Page 37 Exercise D

Is Speaker B answering Yes or No? Listen to each conversation and circle the correct answer.

1. A. Do you know how to drive a bus?
   B. I've driven a bus for many years.
2. A. I usually take the train to work. Do you also take the train?
   B. Actually, I've never taken the train to work.
3. A. Are you a good swimmer?
   B. To tell the truth, I've never swum very well.
4. A. Did you get up early this morning?
   B. I've gotten up early every morning this week.
5. A. I'm going to give my dog a bath today. Do you have any advice?
   B. Sorry. I don't. I've never given my dog a bath.
6. A. Do you like to eat sushi?
   B. Of course! I've eaten sushi for many years.
7. A. I just got a big raise! Did you also get one?
   B. Actually, I've never gotten a raise.
8. A. I did very well on the math exam. How about you?
   B. I've never done well on a math exam.

Page 47 Exercise O

What things have these people done? What haven't they done? Listen and check Yes or No.

1. A. Carla, have you done your homework yet?
   B. Yes, I have. I did my homework this morning.
   A. And have you practiced the violin?
   B. No, I haven't practiced yet. I promise I'll practice this afternoon.
2. A. Kevin?
   B. Yes, Mrs. Blackwell?
   A. Have you written your report yet?
   B. No, I haven't. I'll write it immediately.
   A. And have you sent a fax to the Crane Company?
   B. No, I haven't. I promise I'll send them a fax after I write the report.

3. A. Have you fed the dog yet?
   B. Yes, I have. I fed him a few minutes ago.
   A. Good. Well, I guess we can leave for work now.
   B. But we haven't eaten breakfast yet!
4. A. I'm leaving now, Mr. Green.
   B. Have you fixed the pipes in the basement, Charlie?
   A. Yes, I have.
   B. And have you repaired the washing machine?
   A. Yes, I have. It's working again.
   B. That's great! Thank you, Charlie.
   A. I'll send you a bill, Mr. Green.
5. A. You know, we haven't done the laundry all week.
   B. I know. We should do it today.
   A. We also haven't vacuumed the rugs!
   B. We haven't?
   A. No, we haven't.
   B. Oh. I guess we should vacuum them today.
6. A. Are we ready for the party?
   B. I think so. We've gotten all the food at the supermarket, and we've cleaned the house from top to bottom!
   A. Well, I guess we're ready for the party!
7. A. Have you spoken to the landlord about our broken light?
   B. Yes, I have. I spoke to him this morning.
   A. What did he say?
   B. He said we should call an electrician.
   A. Okay. Let's call Ajax Electric.
   B. Don't worry. I've already called them, and they're coming this afternoon.
8. A. Have you hooked up the new VCR yet?
   B. I can't do it. It's really difficult.
   A. Have you read the instructions?
   B. Yes, I have. I've read them ten times, and I still can't understand them!

Page 56 Exercise E

Listen and choose the correct answer.

1. Bob has been engaged since he got out of the army.
2. My sister Carol has been a professional musician since she finished music school.
3. Michael has been home since he fell and hurt himself last week.
4. My wife has gotten up early every morning since she started her new job.
5. Richard has eaten breakfast in the school cafeteria every morning since he started college.
6. Nancy and Tom have known each other for five and a half years.
7. My friend Charlie and I have played soccer every weekend since we were eight years old.

8. Patty has had short hair since she was a teenager.
9. Ron has owned his own business since he moved to Chicago nine years ago.
10. I've been interested in astronomy for the past eleven years.
11. I use my personal computer all the time. I've had it since I was in high school.
12. Alan has had problems with his house since he bought it fifteen years ago.

Page 61 Exercise L

Listen and choose the correct answer.

1. A. Have you always been a salesperson?
   B. No. I've been a salesperson for the past four years. Before that, I was a cashier.

2. A. How long has your daughter been in medical school?
   B. She's been in medical school for the past two years.

3. A. Have your parents always lived in a house?
   B. No. They've lived in a house for the past ten years. Before that, they lived in an apartment.

4. A. How long have you wanted to be an actor?
   B. I've wanted to be an actor since I was in college. Before that, I wanted to be a musician.

5. A. Do you and your husband still exercise at your health club every day?
   B. No. We haven't done that for a year.

6. A. Has James been a bachelor all his life?
   B. No, he hasn't. He was married for ten years.

7. A. Has your sister Jane always wanted to be a writer?
   B. Yes, she has. She's wanted to be a writer all her life.

8. A. Have you ever broken your ankle?
   B. No. I've sprained it a few times, but I've never broken it.

9. A. Have you always liked classical music?
   B. No. I've liked classical music for the past few years. Before that, I liked rock music.

10. A. Has Billy had a sore throat for a long time?
    B. He's had a sore throat for the past two days. Before that, he had a fever.

11. A. Jennifer has been the store manager since last fall.
    B. What did she do before that?
    A. She was a salesperson.

12. A. Have you always been interested in modern art?
    B. No. I've been interested in modern art since I moved to Paris a few years ago. Before that, I was only interested in sports.

Page 64 Exercise E

Listen and choose the correct time expressions to complete the sentences.

1. A. How long have you been living there?
   B. I've been living there since . . .

2. A. How long has your daughter been practicing the piano?
   B. She's been practicing for . . .

3. A. How long have I been running?
   B. You've been running since . . .

4. A. How long have you been feeling bad?
   B. I've been feeling bad for . . .

5. A. How long have they been waiting?
   B. They've been waiting for . . .

6. A. How long has your son been studying?
   B. He's been studying since . . .

7. A. How long have your sister and her boyfriend been dating?
   B. They've been dating since . . .

8. A. Dad, how long have we been driving?
   B. Hmm. I think we've been driving for . . .

9. A. How long has your little girl been crying?
   B. She's been crying for . . .

Page 67 Exercise H

Listen and choose what the people are talking about.

1. She's been directing it for an hour.
2. We've been rearranging it all morning.
3. I've been paying them on time.
4. He's been playing them for years.
5. Have you been bathing them for a long time?
6. They've been rebuilding it for a year.
7. She's been writing it for a week.
8. He's been translating them for many years.
9. I've been reading it all afternoon.
10. She's been knitting them for a few weeks.
11. We've been listening to them all afternoon.
12. I've been recommending it for years.
13. They've been repairing it all day.
14. She's been taking it all morning.
15. I've been solving them all my life.

Page 71 Exercise L

Listen and decide where the conversation is taking place.

1. A. I'm really tired.
   B. No wonder! You've been chopping tomatoes for the past hour.

2. A. Mark! I'm surprised. You've been falling asleep in class all morning, and you've never fallen asleep in class before.
   B. I'm sorry, Mrs. Applebee. It won't happen again.

Activity Workbook   **A5**

3. A. I've been washing these shirts for the past half hour, and they still aren't clean.
   B. Here. Try this Presto Soap.

4. A. We've been standing in line for an hour and forty-five minutes.
   B. I know. I hope the movie is good. I've never stood in line for such a long time.

5. A. What seems to be the problem, Mr. Jones?
   B. My back has been hurting me for the past few days.
   A. I'm sorry to hear that.

6. A. You know, we've been reading here for more than two hours.
   B. You're right. I think it's time to go now.

7. A. Do you want to leave?
   B. I think so. We've seen all the paintings here.

8. A. How long have you been exercising?
   B. For an hour and a half.

9. A. We've been waiting for an hour, and it still isn't here.
   B. I know. I'm going to be late for work.

10. A. I think we've seen them all. Which one do you want to buy?
    B. I like that black one over there.

11. A. We've been watching this movie for the past hour, and it's terrible!
    B. You're right. Let's change the channel.

12. A. I've got a terrible headache.
    B. Why?
    A. Customers have been complaining all morning.
    B. What have they been complaining about?
    A. Some people have been complaining about our terrible products, but most people have been complaining about our high prices.

Page 77 Exercise F

Listen and choose the correct answer.

1. A. How long has Janet been an actress?
   B. She's been an actress since she graduated from acting school.

2. A. Have you watched the news yet?
   B. Yes. I saw the president, and I heard his speech.

3. A. Have you always lived in Denver?
   B. No. We've lived in Denver since 1995. Before that, we lived in New York.

4. A. Has Dad made dinner yet?
   B. Not yet. He still has to make it.

5. A. How long has your ceiling been leaking?
   B. It's been leaking for more than a week.
   A. Have you called the superintendent?
   B. Yes, I have. I've called him several times.

6. A. Billy is having trouble with his homework.
   B. Has he asked anyone to help him?
   A. No, he hasn't.

Page 87 Exercise N

Listen and choose the correct answer.

1. Dr. Gomez really enjoys . . .
2. Whenever possible, my wife and I try to avoid . . .
3. Next summer I'm going to learn . . .
4. Every day Rita practices . . .
5. My parents have decided . . .
6. I've considered . . .
7. Are you thinking about . . .
8. I'm going to quit . . .
9. Why do you keep on . . .
10. My doctor says I should stop . . .
11. David can't stand . . .
12. Are you going to continue to . . .
13. James doesn't want to start . . .
14. Next semester Kathy is going to begin . . .
15. You know, you can't keep on . . .

Page 97 Exercise J

Listen and choose the correct answer.

1. Steve lost his voice.
2. Is Beverly one of your relatives?
3. We just canceled our trip to South America.
4. Ricky has been failing all of his tests this year.
5. Francine dislocated her shoulder.
6. What did you and your students discuss in class?
7. My girlfriend and I rode on the roller coaster yesterday.
8. Grandma can't chew this piece of steak very well.
9. Jimmy loves my homemade food.
10. Did you see the motorcycles go by?
11. Do you think Mr. Montero will take a day off soon?
12. Amy wanted to ask her boss for a raise, but she got cold feet.
13. Have you heard that Margaret sprained her wrist?
14. I have to make an important decision.
15. I envy you.
16. I feel terrible. Debbie and Dan broke up last week.
17. My ankle hurts a lot.
18. I was heartbroken when I heard what happened.
19. Michael was furious with his neighbors.
20. We went to a recital last night.
21. Tom, don't forget to shine your shoes!
22. My friend Carla is extremely athletic.
23. My husband and I have been writing invitations all afternoon.
24. Charles rented a beautiful tuxedo for his niece's wedding.

Page 99 Exercise D

Listen and choose the correct answer.

Ex. My grandfather likes to . . .
1. Susan says she's going to stop . . .
2. My wife and I are thinking about . . .
3. David is considering . . .
4. I can't stand to . . .
5. You should definitely keep on . . .

Page 105 Exercise G

Listen and choose the correct answer.

1. A. I looked in the refrigerator, and I can't find the orange juice.
   B. That's because we . . .
2. A. I'm frustrated! My computer isn't working today.
   B. I think you forgot to . . .
3. A. What should I do with the Christmas decorations?
   B. I think it's time to . . .
4. A. Should I take these clothes to the cleaner's?
   B. Yes. You should definitely . . .
5. A. Hmm. What does this word mean?
   B. You should . . .
6. A. I have to return this skateboard to my cousin.
   B. When are you going to . . . ?
7. A. This math problem is very difficult.
   B. Maybe I can . . .
8. A. I'll never remember their new telephone number.
   B. You should . . .
9. A. I just spilled milk on the kitchen floor!
   B. Don't worry. I'll . . .

Page 108 Exercise L

Listen and choose the correct answer.

1. I really look up to my father.
2. My brother picks on me all the time.
3. Did you throw away the last can of paint?
4. I still haven't gotten over the flu.
5. Have you heard from your cousin Sam recently?
6. Why did you turn him down?
7. Did your French teacher call on you today?
8. George picked out a new suit for his wedding.
9. I have to drop my sister off at the airport.
10. Everything in the store is 20 percent off this week.
11. This jacket fits you.
12. Did you try on a lot of shoes?

Page 112 Exercise D

Listen and complete the sentences.

1. I missed the bus this morning.
2. I'm allergic to nuts.
3. I'll be on vacation next week.
4. I've never flown in a helicopter.
5. I can speak Chinese.
6. I like to go sailing.
7. I'm not going to the company picnic this weekend.
8. I saw a very good movie last night.
9. I don't go on many business trips.
10. I've been to London several times.
11. I'm not a vegetarian.
12. I should lose a little weight.
13. I can't stop worrying about my health.
14. I hate to drive downtown.
15. I won't be able to go to Nancy's party this Saturday night.

Page 117 Exercise K

Listen and complete the sentences.

1. I missed the bus today, . . .
2. I'm allergic to cats, . . .
3. I'll be on vacation next week, . . .
4. You've never seen a rainbow, . . .
5. I can speak Italian, . . .
6. I like to go sailing, . . .
7. I've been on television several times, . . .
8. I saw an exciting movie last weekend, . . .
9. I won't be in the office tomorrow, . . .
10. We were late, . . .
11. I'm not a vegetarian, . . .
12. I saw the stop sign, . . .
13. I can't swim very well, . . .
14. They have to work overtime this weekend, . . .
15. I won't be able to go to Sam's party this Friday night, . . .
16. I'm not afraid of flying, . . .
17. I haven't eaten breakfast yet, . . .
18. The other students weren't bored, . . .

Page 121 Exercise C

Listen and complete the sentences.

Ex. Nancy knows how to type, . . .
1. I'm interested in science, . . .
2. I won't be home this evening, . . .
3. I own my own business, . . .
4. I've never hooked up a computer, . . .
5. You just got a raise, . . .

UNIT 1

WORKBOOK PAGE 2

A. What's Happening?

1. What's, reading, She's reading
2. Where's, going, He's going
3. What's, watching, She's watching
4. What are, cooking, I'm cooking
5. Where are, moving, We're moving
6. Where are, sitting, They're sitting
7. What's, composing, He's composing
8. What are, baking, I'm baking

WORKBOOK PAGE 3

B. On the Phone

1. are
   I'm watching
   Is
   she is, She's taking
2. Are
   They're
   are they
   is doing
   is playing
   What are you
   I'm cooking
3. Is
   he isn't, He's exercising
   She's, She's fixing

WORKBOOK PAGE 4

C. You Decide: *Why Is Today Different?*

1. clean, I'm cleaning, . . .
2. irons, he's ironing, . . .
3. argue, we're arguing, . . .
4. worry, I'm worrying, . . .
5. watches, she's watching, . . .
6. writes, he's writing, . . .
7. take, I'm taking, . . .
8. combs, he's combing, . . .
9. gets up, she's getting up, . . .
10. smiles, he's smiling, . . .
11. bark, they're barking, . . .
12. wears, she's wearing, . . .

WORKBOOK PAGE 5

D. What Are They Saying?

1. Do you recommend
2. Does, bake

3. Does, get up
4. Do, complain
5. Does, speak
6. Does, live
7. Do you watch
8. Does she play
9. Does he practice
10. Do you plant
11. Does he add
12. Do you wear
13. Does she ride
14. Does he jog
15. Do we need
16. Does he iron
17. Do they have

WORKBOOK PAGE 6

E. Puzzle

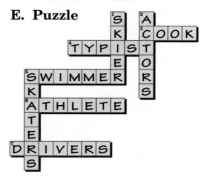

F. What's the Answer?

1. b   5. b
2. c   6. c
3. b   7. a
4. c   8. b

WORKBOOK PAGE 7

G. What Are They Saying?

1. don't, doesn't
   isn't, cook
2. don't, I'm
   drive
3. Do you
   don't, I'm
   You're, type
4. composes, he's
5. isn't, doesn't
   swimmer
6. don't
   speak, speaker

Answers are not provided for the achievement tests. Complete test answer keys are included in *Side by Side Plus* Teacher's Guide 3 and Multilevel Activity & Achievement Test Book 3 (and its accompanying CD-ROM).

Activity Workbook   **A9**

H. Listening

1. he does
2. she isn't
3. they are
4. they do
5. she doesn't
6. it is
7. he isn't
8. I do
9. she doesn't
10. he is
11. I'm not
12. we do
13. she is
14. they aren't
15. we don't

WORKBOOK PAGE 9

J. What's the Question?

1. What are you waiting for?
2. Who is he thinking about?
3. What are they ironing?
4. Who are you calling?
5. Who is she dancing with?
6. What's he watching?
7. What are they complaining about?
8. Who is she playing baseball with?
9. Who are they visiting?
10. What are you looking at?
11. What are you writing about?
12. Who is he arguing with?
13. Who is she knitting a sweater for?
14. What are you making?
15. Who are you sending an e-mail to?
16. What are they worrying about?
17. Who is she talking to?
18. Who is he skating with?

WORKBOOK PAGE 10

K. What Are They Saying?

1. your
   We're, them
2. his
   He, them, his
3. they, me
4. her
   She, them
5. your
   I, my
6. your
   I'm, her
7. They, them
8. us, it
9. he, it
10. your
    She, my

WORKBOOK PAGE 11

L. What's the Word?

1. with
2. —
3. at
4. to
5. about
6. —
7. —, with
8. for
9. —

UNIT 2

WORKBOOK PAGE 12

A. Herbert's Terrible Day!

1. had
2. got up
3. ate
4. rushed
5. ran
6. missed
7. waited
8. decided
9. arrived
10. sat
11. began
12. called
13. typed
14. made
15. fixed
16. finished
17. put
18. spilled
19. went
20. ordered
21. felt
22. forgot
23. crashed
24. fell
25. broke
26. hurt
27. left
28. took
29. went

WORKBOOK PAGE 13

B. Listening

1. every day
2. yesterday
3. every day
4. yesterday
5. every day
6. yesterday
7. yesterday
8. every day
9. yesterday
10. every day
11. every day
12. yesterday

C. What's the Word?

1. wanted
2. lifted
3. painted
4. roller-bladed
5. planted
6. needed
7. waited
8. decided

D. Puzzle: *What Did They Do?*

E. What's the Question?

1. Did you buy
2. Did they take
3. Did she see
4. Did he speak
5. Did you break
6. Did it begin
7. Did she fly
8. Did you have
9. Did they go
10. Did I sing
11. Did he meet
12. Did you lose

F. What's the Answer?

1. they were bored
2. I wasn't hungry
3. they were tired
4. she wasn't prepared
5. he was angry
6. I wasn't on time
7. she wasn't thirsty
8. I was scared
9. they were sad

G. Something Different

1. didn't drive, drove
2. didn't come, came
3. didn't take, took
4. didn't go, went
5. didn't forget, forgot
6. didn't wear, wore
7. didn't teach, taught
8. didn't eat, ate
9. didn't give, gave
10. didn't sit, sat
11. didn't have, had
12. didn't sing, sang

H. What Are They Saying?

1. Did you
   didn't, was
2. Did you
   didn't
   met
3. Did
   did
   wasn't
4. Did
   she didn't
   weren't

5. Did, fall
   he didn't
   fell
   was
6. Did
   I didn't, rode
   was
   was
7. Did you
   did, was
   didn't
   was
8. Was
   was, Were
   I wasn't, didn't
9. Did
   did
   didn't
   were
10. Did
    they didn't
    danced
    were
11. did
    I did, bought
    Did you
    didn't
    wasn't
12. were
    were
    I was, was
    was
    wasn't

I. How Did It Happen?

1. He sprained his ankle while he was playing tennis.
2. She ripped her pants while she was exercising.
3. I broke my arm while I was playing volleyball.
4. He poked himself in the eye while he was fixing his sink.
5. We hurt ourselves while we were skateboarding.
6. They tripped and fell while they were dancing.
7. He burned himself while he was cooking french fries.
8. She got a black eye while she was fighting with the kid across the street.
9. I cut myself while I was chopping carrots.
10. He lost his cell phone while he was jogging in the park.

L. What's the Question?

1. Who did you meet?
2. What did she lose?
3. Where did you do your exercises?
4. When did they leave?
5. How did she get here?
6. Where did he sing?
7. How long did they stay?
8. What kind of movie did you see?
9. Why did he cry?
10. Who did she write a letter to?
11. What did they complain about?
12. How many grapes did you eat?
13. Where did he speak?
14. How long did they lift weights?
15. Who did she give a present to?
16. What kind of pie did you order?
17. How many videos did you rent?
18. Who did they send an e-mail to?
19. When did he fall asleep?
20. When did you lose your hat?

WORKBOOK PAGES 21–22

M. Our Vacation

1. we didn't
   did you go
   We went
2. we didn't
   did you get there
   We got there by plane.
3. it didn't
   did it leave
   It left
4. we didn't
   weather did you have
   We had
5. we didn't
   hotel did you stay in
   We stayed in a small hotel.
6. we didn't
   food did you eat
   We ate Japanese food.
7. we didn't
   did you take (with you)
   We took
8. we didn't
   did you get around the city
   We got around the city by taxi.
9. we didn't
   did you meet
   We met
10. we didn't
    did you buy
    We bought

11. we didn't
    did you speak
    We spoke English.
12. we did
    money did you spend
    We spent . . .

WORKBOOK PAGE 23

N. Sound It Out!

1. these
2. did
3. Rita
4. big
5. green
6. mittens
7. knit
8. Did Rita knit these big green mittens?
9. Greek
10. his
11. Richard
12. every
13. speaks
14. with
15. week
16. sister
17. Richard speaks Greek with his sister every week.

UNIT 3

WORKBOOK PAGE 24

A. What Are They Saying?

1. No, I didn't.
   rode
   I'm going to ride
2. No, he didn't.
   wore
   He's going to wear
3. No, she didn't.
   gave
   She's going to give
4. No, they didn't.
   drove
   They're going to drive
5. No, we didn't.
   had
   We're going to have
6. No, I didn't.
   went
   I'm going to go

7. No, he didn't.
   wrote
   He's going to write
8. No, she didn't.
   left
   She's going to leave

WORKBOOK PAGES 25–26

B. Bad Connections!

1. your dentist going to do
2. are you going to go
3. is she going to move to Alaska
4. What are they going to give you?
5. What are you going to do?
6. When are you going to get married?
7. Who are you going to meet?
8. What are you going to name your new puppy?
9. Why are they going to sell your house?
10. Where are you going to go?
11. Who do you have to call?
12. Why are you going to fire me?

C. Listening

1. b
2. a
3. a
4. b
5. a
6. b
7. b
8. a
9. a
10. b
11. b
12. a

WORKBOOK PAGE 27

D. The Pessimist and the Optimists

1. won't have   you will, You'll
2. will hurt   he won't, He won't
3. won't   she will, She'll
4. will be   she won't, She won't
5. won't lose   you will, You'll
6. will forget   they won't, They won't
7. won't fix   he will, He'll
8. won't   they will, They'll like
9. I'll   you won't, You won't

WORKBOOK PAGE 28

E. What Will Be Happening?

1. she will, She'll be doing
2. I will, I'll be filling out
3. he won't, He'll be working out
4. they will, They'll be cleaning
5. he will, He'll be browsing
6. we will, We'll be watching
7. she won't, She'll be attending
8. it won't, It'll be raining

WORKBOOK PAGE 29

G. What Are They Saying?

1. giving, will you be giving

2. will you be doing, be doing
3. talk, talk, studying
4. having/eating, will you be having/eating

WORKBOOK PAGE 31

I. Whose Is It?

1. yours
2. mine
3. his
4. hers
5. theirs
6. ours
7. hers
8. hers

WORKBOOK PAGES 32–33

K. What Does It Mean?

1. b
2. c
3. b
4. b
5. a
6. a
7. c
8. b
9. a
10. c
11. a
12. c
13. a
14. b
15. a
16. b
17. a
18. b
19. c
20. a
21. c
22. a
23. b
24. c

L. Listening: *Looking Forward*

1. a
2. c
3. b
4. b
5. c
6. b
7. b
8. a
9. c

WORKBOOK PAGES 34–35

CHECK-UP TEST: Units 1–3

A.
1. are
   dance
2. drives
3. you're
   swimmers
4. I'm
   typist
5. aren't, skiers

B.
1. didn't, was
   spoke
2. didn't
   bought
3. Did
   didn't, got
4. didn't, taught
   was
5. Did
   didn't, talked
   wasn't

C.
1. What are you writing about?
2. What are they going to fix?
3. Where did he hike?
4. When will she be ready?
5. How did they arrive?
6. How long will you be staying?
7. How many people is she going to hire?

D.

1. She's adjusting her satellite dish.
2. He chats online.
3. I'm going to visit my mother-in-law.
4. They delivered groceries.
5. He was baking a cake.
6. I'll take the bus.
7. We'll be watching TV.
8. I was chopping carrots.

E.

1. I am
2. they won't
3. you did
4. he does
5. she isn't
6. we do
7. she doesn't
8. we will

UNIT 4

WORKBOOK PAGE 36

A. For Many Years

1. I've ridden
2. I've flown
3. I've given
4. I've spoken
5. I've taken
6. I've done
7. I've drawn
8. I've written
9. I've driven

B. Listening

1. a
2. b
3. a
4. b
5. b
6. a
7. a
8. b

WORKBOOK PAGE 37

C. I've Never

1. I've never flown
2. I've never gotten
3. I've never ridden
4. I've never drawn
5. I've never written
6. I've never taken
7. I've never sung
8. I've never swum
9. I've never been
10. I've never gone
11. I've never given
12. I've never seen

D. Listening

1. Yes
2. No
3. No
4. Yes
5. No
6. Yes
7. No
8. No

WORKBOOK PAGE 38

E. What Are They Saying?

1. Have you ever gotten
   I got
2. Have you ever ridden
   I rode
3. Have you ever worn
   I wore
4. Have you ever gone
   I went
5. Have you ever given
   I gave
6. Have you ever fallen
   I fell

WORKBOOK PAGE 39

G. What Are They Saying?

1. Have, eaten
   they have, They ate
2. Has, driven
   he has, He drove
3. Has, gone
   she has, She went
4. Have, seen
   we have, We saw
5. Have, taken
   they have, They took
6. Have, spoken
   I have, I spoke
7. Have, written
   you have, You wrote
8. Have, met
   we have, We met

WORKBOOK PAGE 40

H. Not Today

1. They've, eaten
   They ate
2. She's, gone
   She went
3. He's, worn
   He wore
4. We've, done
   We did
5. He's, given
   He gave
6. I've, seen
   I saw
7. We've, bought
   We bought
8. She's, visited
   She visited
9. He's, taken
   He took

WORKBOOK PAGE 41

I. What's the Word?

1. go
2. went
3. gone
4. seen
5. saw
6. see
7. ate
8. eaten
9. eat
10. write
11. written
12. wrote
13. wear
14. worn
15. wore
16. spoke

A14   **Activity Workbook**

17. speak
18. spoken
19. driven
20. drive
21. drove
22. do
23. did
24. done

WORKBOOK PAGES 42–43

J. What Are They Saying?

1. I've, done
   I did
   have, written
   I have
2. I've, swum
   I swam
3. I've, taken
   I took
   Have, taken
   I have, took
4. He's, gotten
   He got
5. We've, eaten
   We ate
   eaten
6. I've, spoken
   I spoke

WORKBOOK PAGES 44–45

L. In a Long Time

1. I haven't ridden
2. haven't bought
3. I haven't flown
4. I haven't taken
5. I haven't swum
6. hasn't eaten
7. hasn't cleaned
8. He hasn't read
9. I haven't studied
10. haven't seen
11. I haven't given
12. He hasn't made
13. haven't gone
14. I haven't danced

M. Puzzle: *What Have They Already Done?*

WORKBOOK PAGES 46–47

N. A Lot of Things to Do

1. He's already gone to the supermarket.
2. He hasn't cleaned his apartment yet.
3. He's already gotten a haircut.
4. He hasn't baked a cake yet.
5. He's already fixed his CD player.
6. She's already taken a shower.
7. She hasn't done her exercises yet.
8. She hasn't fed the cat yet.
9. She's already walked the dog.
10. She hasn't eaten breakfast yet.
11. They haven't done their laundry yet.
12. They've already gotten their paychecks.
13. They've already paid their bills.
14. They haven't packed their suitcases yet.
15. They haven't said good-bye to their friends yet.
16. She's already written to Mrs. Lane.
17. She's already called Mr. Sanchez.
18. She hasn't met with Ms. Wong yet.
19. She hasn't read her e-mail yet.
20. She's already sent a fax to the Ace Company.

O. Listening

	Yes	No		Yes	No
1.	✔	___	5.	___	✔
	___	✔		___	✔
2.	___	✔	6.	✔	___
	___	✔		___	✔
3.	✔	___	7.	✔	___
	___	✔		___	✔
4.	✔	___	8.	___	✔
	✔	___		✔	___

WORKBOOK PAGES 48–49

P. What Are They Saying?

1. have, spoke
   did
   flown
2. Have
   haven't, saw
   see
   seen
3. taken
   took
   Have, sent
   sent
   Have, given
4. Have
   have, went
   Have, gone/been
   have, I went/was

5. did
gave
are you going to buy
spent
did you
bought
listen
6. I'm not, taken
got
Have
I have, ate
washed/done

WORKBOOK PAGE 50

R. *J*ulia's Broken Keyboard

1.

> *J*udy,
>
> Have you seen my blue and *y*ellow *j*acket at *y*our house? I think I left it there *y*esterday after the *j*azz concert. I've looked everywhere, and I *j*ust can't find it anywhere.
>
> *J*ulia

2.

> Dear *J*ennifer,
>
> We're sorry *y*ou haven't been able to visit us this *y*ear. Do *y*ou think *y*ou could come in *J*une or *J*uly? We really en*j*oyed *y*our visit last *y*ear. We really want to see *y*ou again.
>
> *J*ulia

3.

> *J*eff,
>
> *J*ack and I have gone out *j*ogging, but we'll be back in *j*ust a few minutes. Make *y*ourself comfortable. *Y*ou can wait for us in the *y*ard. We haven't eaten lunch *y*et. We'll have some *y*ogurt and orange *j*uice when we get back.
>
> *J*ulia

4.

> Dear *J*ane,
>
> We *j*ust received the beautiful pa*j*amas *y*ou sent to *J*immy. Thank *y*ou very much. *J*immy is too *y*oung to write to *y*ou himself, but he says "Thank *y*ou." He's already worn the pa*j*amas, and he's en*j*oying them a lot.
>
> *J*ulia

5.

> Dear *J*anet,
>
> *J*ack and I are coming to visit *y*ou and *J*ohn in New *Y*ork. We've been to New *Y*ork before, but we haven't visited the Statue of Liberty or the Empire State Building *y*et. See *y*ou in *J*anuary or maybe in *J*une.
>
> *J*ulia

6.

> Dear *J*oe,
>
> We got a letter from *J*ames last week. He has en*j*oyed college a lot this *y*ear. His favorite sub*j*ects are German and *J*apanese. He's looking for a *j*ob as a *j*ournalist in *J*apan, but he hasn't found one *y*et.
>
> *J*ulia

WORKBOOK PAGE 51

S. *Is or Has?*

1. has	**11.** is
2. is	**12.** has
3. is	**13.** is
4. has	**14.** has
5. is	**15.** has
6. is	**16.** is
7. has	**17.** has
8. is	**18.** is
9. is	**19.** is
10. has	**20.** has

UNIT 5

WORKBOOK PAGE 52

A. How Long?

1. I've had a headache since
2. They've been married for
3. He's owned a motorcycle since
4. She's been interested in astronomy for
5. I've had a cell phone since
6. We've known each other since
7. They've had a dog for
8. I've had problems with my upstairs neighbor for
9. She's been a computer programmer since
10. He's played in the school orchestra since
11. There have been mice in our attic for

WORKBOOK PAGE 53

B. What's the Question?

1. How long has, wanted to be an engineer
2. How long has, owned his own house
3. How long have, been married
4. How long have, been interested in photography
5. How long has, worn glasses
6. How long have, known how to snowboard
7. How long has, had a girlfriend
8. How long has, been a pizza shop in town

WORKBOOK PAGE 55

D. Since When?

1. I'm
   I've been sick

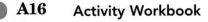

A16   **Activity Workbook**

2. has
   She's had
3. knows
   He's known
4. They're
   They've been
5. We're
   We've been
6. have
   I've had
7. It's
   It's been
8. plays
   She's
9. is
   He's been
10. I'm
    I've been

WORKBOOK PAGE 56

E. Listening

1. b		7. a	
2. b		8. b	
3. a		9. b	
4. b		10. a	
5. a		11. b	
6. a		12. a	

F. Crossword

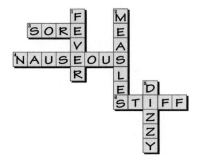

WORKBOOK PAGE 57

G. Scrambled Sentences

1. Julie has liked jazz since she was a teenager.
2. He's known how to play the piano since he was a little boy.
3. I've been interested in astronomy since I was young.
4. They've been engaged since they finished college.
5. He's been a chef since he graduated from cooking school.
6. She's wanted to be a teacher since she was eighteen years old.
7. They've owned their own business since they moved here a year ago.

WORKBOOK PAGE 58

I. Then and Now

1. walk
   They've walked
   they
   walked
2. speaks
   He's spoken
   he spoke
3. is
   She's been
   she was
4. taught
   he teaches
   He's taught
5. has
   visited
   visited
   visit
6. has
   She's had
   had

WORKBOOK PAGE 59

J. Looking Back

1. has Victor been
   He's been a musician, 1990
2. was he
   He was a photographer, 7 years
3. has Mrs. Sanchez taught
   She's taught science, 1995
4. did she teach
   She taught math, 9 years
5. did your grandparents have
   They had a cat, 11 years
6. have they had
   They've had a dog, 1998
7. has Betty worked
   She's worked at the bank, 2000
8. did she work
   She worked at the mall, 2 years
9. did your parents live
   They lived in New York, 20 years
10. have they lived
    They've lived in Miami, 2001

WORKBOOK PAGE 61

L. Listening

1. b		7. b	
2. b		8. a	
3. a		9. b	
4. b		10. b	
5. b		11. b	
6. a		12. a	

Activity Workbook **A17**

UNIT 6

WORKBOOK PAGE 62

A. What's the Word?

1. since
2. for
3. for
4. since
5. since
6. for
7. since
8. for

B. Choose

1. a
2. b
3. b
4. a
5. b
6. b

WORKBOOK PAGE 63

C. How Long?

1. I've been studying since
2. She's been feeling sick for
3. He's been having problems with his car for
4. They've been arguing since
5. We've been waiting for
6. It's been ringing since
7. He's been talking for
8. They've been dating since
9. I've been teaching since
10. You've been chatting online for

WORKBOOK PAGE 64

D. What Are They Doing?

1. is looking
   He's been looking
2. is jogging
   She's been jogging
3. is barking
   It's been barking
4. are planting
   They've been planting
5. is doing
   He's been doing
6. is browsing
   She's been browsing
7. are assembling
   They've been assembling
8. baking
   I've been baking
9. are making
   You've been making

E. Listening

1. a
2. b
3. a
4. b
5. b
6. a
7. b
8. a
9. b

WORKBOOK PAGES 66–67

G. What Are They Saying?

1. Have you been waiting
   have
   I've been waiting
2. Has it been snowing
   it has
   It's been snowing
3. Has he been taking
   he has
   He's been taking
4. Have you been working
   I haven't
   been working
5. Has, been making
   it has
   It's been making
6. Have you been vacuuming
   I have
   I've been vacuuming
7. Have they been studying
   they have
   They've been studying
8. Have we been running
   have
   We've been running
9. Have you been wearing
   I haven't
   I've been wearing
10. Have you been playing
    I haven't
    I've been playing

H. Listening

1. a
2. b
3. b
4. a
5. b
6. b
7. a
8. a
9. b
10. a
11. b
12. a
13. b
14. a
15. b

WORKBOOK PAGE 68

I. Sound It Out!

1. interested
2. is
3. Steve's
4. in
5. history
6. sister
7. very
8. Chinese
9. Steve's sister is very interested in Chinese history.

10. receive
11. this
12. any
13. Peter
14. week
15. didn't
16. e-mail
17. Peter didn't receive any e-mail this week.

WORKBOOK PAGES 70–71

K. What's Happening?

1. We've been eating
   We've, eaten
   We haven't eaten
2. She's been seeing
   She's, see
   She hasn't seen
3. He's been swimming
   He's, swum
4. She's been going
   She's, gone
5. He's been talking
   He's, talked
   he hasn't talked
6. They've been writing
   They've, written
   they haven't written
7. he's been making
   He's, made
   He hasn't made
8. She's been studying
   She's, studied
   she hasn't studied
9. He's been reading
   He's, read
   he hasn't read
10. They've been
    complaining
    They've, complained
    haven't complained

L. Listening

1. a		7. b
2. b		8. a
3. b		9. b
4. a		10. b
5. a		11. a
6. b		12. b

WORKBOOK PAGE 72

M. Which Word?

1. leaking	7. given
2. flying	8. taken
3. run	9. gone
4. made	10. has been ringing
5. have you been	11. singing
6. see	

WORKBOOK PAGE 74

O. A New Life

1. He's never lived in a big city
2. He's never taken English lessons
3. He's never taken the subway
4. He's never shopped in American supermarkets
5. He's never eaten American food
6. He's never played American football

8. They've been living in a big city
9. They've been taking English lessons
10. They've been taking the subway
11. They've been shopping in American supermarkets
12. They've been eating American food
13. They've been playing American football

WORKBOOK PAGES 76–77

CHECK-UP TEST: Units 4–6

A.

1. have, eaten	4. has, gone
2. hasn't taken	5. haven't paid
3. haven't written	6. has, had

B.

1. Have you spoken	4. Has he, flown
2. Has he ridden	5. Has she, been
3. Have they gotten	6. Have you met

C.

1. It's been sunny	5. They've been arguing
2. We've been browsing	6. I've known
3. She's had	7. She's been
4. He's been studying	8. We've been cleaning

D.

1. She's been working at the bank since
2. They've been barking for
3. It's been snowing for
4. I've wanted to be an astronaut since

E.

1. He's owned
   he owned
2. I've been
   I was
3. She's liked
   she liked

F.

1. b	4. a
2. a	5. a
3. b	6. b

WORKBOOK PAGE 78

A. What Do They ${ \text{Enjoy Doing} \atop \text{Like to Do} }$?

1. enjoy
2. likes to, Talking
3. enjoy
4. like to, Knitting
5. enjoy
6. likes to, delivering
7. enjoy, being
8. likes to, planting
9. enjoys, chatting
10. like to, playing
11. enjoy
12. likes to, going
13. enjoy

WORKBOOK PAGE 80

C. What's the Word?

1. complain
2. sitting
3. eat
4. clean
5. wear
6. cleaning
7. go
8. going
9. sit
10. complaining
11. eating
12. wearing

WORKBOOK PAGE 82

F. My Energetic Grandfather

1. to play/playing
2. to play
3. play

WORKBOOK PAGE 83

H. Choose

1. to buy
2. moving
3. going
4. changing
5. get
6. retiring

WORKBOOK PAGE 85

K. What's the Word?

1. rearranging
2. eating
3. worrying
4. to get/getting
5. to exercise/exercising
6. to ask/asking
7. arguing
8. to take/taking

9. paying, to pay/paying
10. to fall/falling

L. Good Decisions

1. biting
2. to do/doing
3. to cook
4. to cook/cooking
5. paying
6. cleaning
7. gossiping
8. interrupting

WORKBOOK PAGE 86

M. Problems!

1. falling
   falling
2. to lift/lifting
   to lift/lifting
   lifting
3. to tease/teasing
   teasing
   crying
   teasing
4. driving
   to drive/driving
   to drive/driving
5. dressing
   to dress/dressing
   dressing
6. stepping
   to dance/dancing
   going

WORKBOOK PAGE 87

N. Listening

1. a
2. a
3. b
4. b
5. a
6. a
7. b
8. b
9. a
10. b
11. b
12. b
13. a
14. a
15. b

O. What Does It Mean?

1. b
2. c
3. a
4. b
5. c
6. a
7. b
8. a
9. c
10. b
11. b
12. c

WORKBOOK PAGE 88

A. Before

1. had eaten
2. had, gotten
3. had, visited
4. had driven
5. had, cut
6. had spent
7. had, gone
8. had made
9. had seen
10. had, left
11. had had
12. had, given
13. had lost

WORKBOOK PAGE 90

C. Late for Everything

1. had, left
2. had, begun
3. had, gone---
4. had, closed
5. had, started
6. had, left
7. had, arrived

WORKBOOK PAGE 91

D. In a Long Time

1. hadn't listened
2. hadn't seen
3. hadn't had
4. hadn't gone
5. hadn't remembered
6. hadn't ironed, hadn't shaved
7. hadn't lost
8. hadn't skied
9. hadn't gotten
10. hadn't taken off
11. hadn't studied
12. hadn't ridden

WORKBOOK PAGES 92–93

E. Working Hard

1. She was studying for her science test.
2. She had already written an English composition.
3. She hadn't practiced the trombone yet.
4. She hadn't read the next history chapter yet.
5. She hadn't memorized her lines for the school play yet.
6. He was hooking up the new printer.
7. He had already sent an e-mail to the boss.
8. He had already given the employees their paychecks.

9. He hadn't written to the Bentley Company yet.
10. He hadn't taken two packages to the post office yet.
11. They were cleaning the garage.
12. They had already assembled Billy's new bicycle.
13. They had already fixed the fence.
14. They hadn't repaired the roof yet.
15. They hadn't started to build a tree house yet.
16. She was playing squash.
17. She had already done yoga.
18. She had already gone jogging
19. She hadn't lifted weights yet.
20. She hadn't swum across the pool 10 times yet.

WORKBOOK PAGE 94

F. What Had They Been Doing?

1. had been talking
2. had been living
3. had been working
4. had been going out
5. had been planning
6. had been thinking about
7. had been getting
8. had been borrowing
9. had been eating
10. had been rehearsing
11. had been looking forward
12. had been training
13. had been arriving

WORKBOOK PAGE 96

I. Marylou's Broken Keyboard

1.
> Roger,
>
> I'm afraid there's something wrong with the fireplace in the living room. Also, the refrigerator is broken. I've been calling the landlord for three days on his cell phone, but he hasn't called back. I hope he calls me tomorrow.
>
> Marylou

2.
> Louise,
>
> I'm terribly worried about my brother Larry's health. He hurt his leg while he was playing baseball. He had already dislocated his shoulder while he was surfing last Friday. According to his doctor, he is also having problems with his blood pressure and with his right wrist. He really should try to relax and take life a little easier.
>
> Marylou

3.

Arnold,

Can you possibly recommend a good restaurant in your neighborhood? I'm planning on taking my relatives to lunch tomorrow, but I'm not sure where.

We ate at a very nice Greek restaurant near your apartment building last month, but I haven't been able to remember the name. Do you know the place?

Your friend,
Marylou

4.

Rosa,

I have been planning a trip to Florida. I'll be flying to Orlando on Friday, and I'll be returning three days later. Have you ever been there? I remember you had family members who lived in Florida several years ago.

Please write back.

All my love,
Marylou

WORKBOOK PAGE 97

J. Listening

1.	c	13.	b
2.	b	14.	a
3.	c	15.	c
4.	b	16.	c
5.	c	17.	b
6.	b	18.	c
7.	a	19.	b
8.	b	20.	a
9.	c	21.	b
10.	b	22.	c
11.	a	23.	a
12.	c	24.	c

WORKBOOK PAGES 98–99

CHECK-UP TEST: Units 7–8

A.

1. eating
2. wrestling
3. to stop
4. boxing
5. Swimming
6. to skate
7. talking
8. doing

B.

1. hadn't spoken
2. had, done
3. had, left
4. hadn't written
5. hadn't had
6. hadn't taken
7. hadn't eaten
8. hadn't gone

C.

1. had been working
2. had been training
3. had been arguing
4. had been planning

D.

1. b
2. a
3. b
4. b
5. a

UNIT 9

WORKBOOK PAGE 100

A. What Are They Saying?

1. pick him up
2. turned it on
3. take them back
4. fill them out
5. hang it up
6. hook it up
7. throw them out
8. took it back
9. took them down
10. call her up

WORKBOOK PAGE 101

B. What Are They Saying?

1. turn on
   turn it on
2. hand, in
   hand it in
3. wake up
   wake them up
4. turn, off
   turn it off
5. take off
   take them off
6. put, away
   put them away
7. Put, on
   put them on
8. bring, back
   bring her back

WORKBOOK PAGE 103

D. What Are They Saying?

1. do it over
2. gave it back
3. hook it up
4. think it over

5. look it up
6. turn him down
7. throw them away
8. written it down
9. cross them out
10. turned it off

WORKBOOK PAGE 104
E. What's the Word?

1. put away
2. hook up
3. take back
4. wake up
5. call up
6. write down
7. clean up
8. put away
9. throw out
10. hang up

WORKBOOK PAGE 105
F. What Should They Do?

1. think it over
2. give it back
3. used it up
4. look it up
5. figure it out
6. wake them up
7. turn it off
8. throw them out

G. Listening

1. b		6. a	
2. b		7. b	
3. a		8. a	
4. b		9. b	
5. b			

WORKBOOK PAGE 106
H. Come Up With the Right Answer

1. take after
   take after him
2. heard from
   hear from him
3. called on
   call on me
4. looking through
   looked through them
5. got over
   got over it
6. look up to
   look up to me
7. ran into
   ran into her

8. get along with
   get along with her
9. picks on
   picks on them

WORKBOOK PAGE 107
J. Choose

1. b		8. a	
2. a		9. a	
3. b		10. b	
4. b		11. a	
5. a		12. a	
6. b		13. b	
7. b		14. b	

WORKBOOK PAGE 108
K. What Does It Mean?

1. b		5. a	
2. c		6. a	
3. b		7. b	
4. c		8. c	

L. Listening

1. c		7. a	
2. b		8. c	
3. c		9. c	
4. a		10. b	
5. b		11. a	
6. c		12. b	

UNIT 10

WORKBOOK PAGE 109
A. Not the Only One

1. did I
2. I do
3. can I
4. I am
5. I will
6. was I
7. am I
8. I have
9. I did
10. will I
11. do I

WORKBOOK PAGE 110
B. What a Coincidence!

1. do I
2. I do
3. I did
4. have I
5. I will
6. did I
7. I was
8. I did
9. I am
10. do I
11. am I

WORKBOOK PAGE 111

C. Not the Only One

1. did I
2. I'm not
3. was I
4. I can't
5. I won't
6. have I
7. I can't
8. am I
9. I didn't
10. do I
11. will I

WORKBOOK PAGE 112

D. Listening

1. did I
2. I am
3. will I
4. I haven't
5. I can
6. I do
7. am I
8. I did
9. do I
10. have I
11. I'm not
12. I should
13. can I
14. do I
15. I won't

WORKBOOK PAGE 113

G. What Are They Saying?

1. did he
2. will she
3. he was
4. has she
5. you should
6. they were
7. so can
8. did he
9. I do
10. . . ., so has

WORKBOOK PAGE 114

H. What Are They Saying?

1. can I
2. they didn't
3. is he
4. she doesn't
5. were they
6. she hasn't
7. will they

8. aren't either
9. neither has
10. she hadn't

WORKBOOK PAGE 115

I. What Are They Saying?

1. so did she
   she did, too
2. neither could he
   he couldn't either
3. so does he
   he does, too
4. neither does she
   she doesn't either
5. neither had she
   she hadn't either
6. so is he
   he is, too

WORKBOOK PAGE 116

J. Our Family

1. aren't, been
2. is, playing, doing
3. can, drawing, was
4. doesn't, going
5. isn't, has been taking
6. haven't, lived, for, lived
7. doesn't, hasn't spoken
8. won't, hasn't
9. does, sung, since
10. aren't, up, away
11. doesn't, for
12. aren't, skating, had, skated

WORKBOOK PAGE 117

K. Listening

1. didn't
2. isn't
3. won't
4. have
5. can't
6. doesn't
7. haven't
8. didn't
9. will
10. wasn't
11. is
12. didn't
13. can
14. don't
15. will
16. is
17. have
18. was

M. Sound It Out!

1. cooks
2. too
3. shouldn't
4. put
5. cookies
6. good
7. sugar
8. Good cooks shouldn't put too much sugar in their cookies.
9. two
10. books
11. bookcase
12. who
13. took
14. afternoon
15. Susan's
16. Who took two books from Susan's bookcase this afternoon?

N. What Does It Mean?

1. j	14. a
2. c	15. u
3. q	16. l
4. s	17. p
5. n	18. e
6. h	19. o
7. i	20. k
8. x	21. f
9. m	22. t
10. v	23. z
11. w	24. g
12. y	25. d
13. b	26. r

CHECK-UP TEST: Units 9–10

A.

1. it in
2. up to him
3. from her
4. it over
5. it up
6. out of it
7. for it
8. them up
9. them out
10. it down
11. over it

B.

1. so is
2. neither will
3. were, too
4. can't either
5. so have
6. did, too
7. neither has
8. so do
9. neither is

C.

1. isn't
2. will
3. doesn't
4. has
5. didn't

Correlation Key

Student Text Pages	Activity Workbook Pages	Student Text Pages	Activity Workbook Pages
Chapter 1		**Chapter 7**	
2	2–3	82	78–79
3	4–5	84	80–81
4	6–8	86–87	82
7–8	9–11	88–89	83–84
	T1–T4 (Test)	90–91	85–87
			T31–T36 (Test)
Chapter 2		**Chapter 8**	
12	12–13	96–97	88–89
13	14–17	100	90
14–15	18–19	101	91
18–19	20–23	104–105	92–93
	T5–T10 (Test)	106–107	94–96
		109	97
Chapter 3			T37–T42 (Test)
22–23	24–26	**Check-Up Test**	**98–99**
25	27	**Chapter 9**	
26	28–29	116	100
27	30	117	101–102
28–29	31–33	119	103
	T11–T14 (Test)	122–123	104–105
Check-Up Test	**34–35**	124	106–107
Chapter 4		126–127	108
38	36		T43–T48 (Test)
39	37	**Chapter 10**	
40	38	132	109–110
41	39	133	111–112
42–43	40–43	134–135	113
45	44–45	138–139	114–115
46	46–47	141	116–117
48	48–50	143	118–119
50	51		T49–T54 (Test)
	T15–T18 (Test)	**Check-Up Test**	**120–121**
Chapter 5			
52–53	52–54		
56–57	55–57		
58–59	58–59		
62–63	60–61		
	T19–T24 (Test)		
Chapter 6			
70–71	62–65		
72	66–68		
74–75	69–71		
76–77	72–75		
	T25–T30 (Test)		
Check-Up Test	**76–77**		

SIDE by SIDE Activity Workbook Audio Program

The *Side by Side* Activity Workbook Audio CDs contain all workbook listening activities and GrammarRaps for entertaining language practice through rhythm, stress, and intonation. Students can use the Audio Program to extend their language learning through self-study outside the classroom.

Audio Program Contents